WHAT'S SO
IMPORTANT
ABOUT THE
CROSS

DEREK PRINCE

WHAT'S SO IMPORTANT ABOUT THE CROSS

WHITAKER
HOUSE

Publisher's Note: This book was compiled from the extensive archive of Derek Prince's unpublished materials and approved by the Derek Prince Ministries editorial team.

Unless otherwise indicated, all Scripture quotations are taken from the *New King James Version,* © 1979, 1980, 1982 by Thomas Nelson, Inc. Used by permission. All rights reserved. Scripture quotations marked (KJV) are taken from the King James Version of the Holy Bible. The Scripture quotation referenced *New English Bible* is © 1961, 1970 by Oxford University Press and Cambridge University Press. All rights reserved. The Scripture quotation referenced Weymouth is taken from *The New Testament in Modern Speech: An Idiomatic Translation into Everyday English from the Text of "The Resultant Greek Testament"* by R. F. (Richard Francis) Weymouth.

The pronoun "Himself" relating to Jesus that occurs in a Scripture quotation from the King James Version has been capitalized to correspond to the style used in this book. The forms LORD and GOD (in small caps) in Bible quotations represent the Hebrew name for God *Yahweh* (Jehovah), while Lord and God normally represent the name *Adonai,* in accordance with the Bible version used. Boldface type in the Scripture quotations indicates the author's emphasis.

What's So Important About the Cross?

Derek Prince Ministries
P.O. Box 19501
Charlotte, North Carolina 28219-9501
www.derekprince.org

ISBN: 978-1-62911-802-4
eBook 978-1-62911-803-1
Printed in the United States of America
© 2017 by Derek Prince Ministries–International

Whitaker House
1030 Hunt Valley Circle
New Kensington, PA 15068
www.whitakerhouse.com

Library of Congress Cataloging-in-Publication Data

Names: Prince, Derek, author.
Title: What's so important about the cross? / Derek Prince.
Description: New Kensington, PA : Whitaker House, 2017.
Identifiers: LCCN 2016059239 (print) | LCCN 2017004471 (ebook) | ISBN 9781629118024 (trade pbk. : alk. paper) | ISBN 9781629118031 (E-book)
Subjects: LCSH: Jesus Christ—Crucifixion.
Classification: LCC BT450 .P76 2017 (print) | LCC BT450 (ebook) | DDC 232.96/3—dc23
LC record available at https://lccn.loc.gov/2016059239

3 4 5 6 7 8 9 10 11 12 13 **LLJ** 26 25 24 23 22 21 20 19 18

CONTENTS

THE SOURCE OF GOD'S BLESSINGS AND MERCY

Some years ago, I was in Singapore ministering with a friend, Ross Paterson, who is the head of the Derek Prince Ministries outreach to China. Between sessions, we were walking together in a shopping district. We had stopped in front of one particular shop window, looking casually at some of the items displayed there without any real thought of purchasing anything. Spontaneously, Ross said to me, "The church has got so many things in its shop window today that it has lost sight of the cross."

At the moment Ross said those words, I thought to myself, *How very true*. Later, as I meditated on his observation, it gripped me. I saw how the church has put so many other items in its "window." There is so much being presented to the church—teaching on how to be healed and delivered, how to prosper, how to prophesy, how to be a good father, how to have a strong marriage, and so forth.

I am not being critical of such teaching, because I, myself, have taught on many such themes. However, the point to remember is that none of these how-tos work without the cross. We must never forget that the only source of every blessing and every mercy of God is *the cross of Jesus Christ*. If we are diverted from the centrality of the cross, all other blessings cease to have any real significance.

Apart from the cross, we have a lot of fine principles, ethics, and rules—most of which we fail to live up to. Then, when we find we cannot live up to our principles, we gradually bring them down to our own level. Let me remind you that "our level" does not match the standards of the New Testament. Ultimately, life at our level has no eternal value to us.

So what must we do instead? We must first appreciate the importance of keeping the cross at the center of all that we do and are. In this book, I intend to outline the truth that the cross must be at the center of every aspect of our faith in Christ. Once we establish this foundation, we will go on to examine how to apply this truth in a practical way to the entirety of our lives.

PART ONE

THE CROSS
AT THE CENTER

CHAPTER 1

THE CROSS
AND HUMAN WISDOM

The apostle Paul was acutely aware of the need to keep the cross at the center of one's life. He expressed this in his first letter to the new Christians who made up the church in Corinth. I particularly enjoy the first two chapters of 1 Corinthians because they deal with the difference between the wisdom of this world and the message of the cross.

When Paul wrote about wisdom, he had in mind the Greek philosophy of his day. Before I became a Christian, I studied Greek philosophy at Cambridge University for seven years. Consequently, I understand how true and appropriate Paul's words are about Greek philosophy and human wisdom in general.

AN ASTONISHING OBJECTIVE

It is very clear from Paul's writings that he was a highly educated man with a thorough understanding of Greek philosophy. In addition, he was extremely well educated in the teachings of Judaism in his day.

With this as background, let us read a passage from 1 Corinthians 2:

> *And I, brethren, when I came to you, did not come with excellence of speech or of wisdom declaring to you the testimony of God. For I determined not to know anything among you except Jesus Christ and Him crucified. I was with you in weakness, in fear, and in much trembling. And my speech and my preaching were not with persuasive words of human wisdom, but in demonstration of the Spirit and of power, that your faith should not be in the wisdom of men but in the power of God.*
>
> (1 Corinthians 2:1–5)

Here Paul makes a most astonishing declaration: "*I determined **not to know anything**....*" This would be an unusual statement for any person to make. But for a Jewish person, it is especially astonishing—because, through the centuries, Jews have prized knowledge. For a highly educated Jew to say, "*I determined not to know anything,*" we must ask a pointed question: *What could possibly have caused Paul to make such a decision?*

Before we can answer that question, we must understand the historical setting in which Paul lived. Paul's ministry in Corinth is described in Acts 18. But in the previous chapter, we have the record of Paul's ministry in Athens. At that time, Athens was the university city of the world. It was the center of philosophy and human wisdom—the source of what we have come to call "secular humanism."

In Athens, rather surprisingly I think, Paul adjusted himself to his audience. When he spoke at the Areopagus in Acts 17, he was communicating with those who were in the upper level of the intellectual and social life of the city. Accordingly, he addressed them in terms of philosophy, even quoting a Greek poet. However, in the end, the results of his address were pretty meager, as the final verses of Acts 17 attest. Only a few people believed. It is a matter of debate as to whether Paul took the right or wrong approach in his message at the Areopagus.

Leaving Athens, Paul next went to Corinth, which was a large port city. Typical of a port city, it was full of all sorts of vice: prostitution, homosexuality, immorality, and extortion of every kind. Somewhere between Athens and Corinth, Paul evidently made this decision: "When I get to Corinth, I'm going to forget everything I knew except Jesus Christ, and Him crucified."

The result of Paul's ministry in Corinth was tremendous. The whole city was stirred. Historians estimate that quite early in Corinth's Christian community, there were probably twenty-five thousand believers. Those numbers represent a totally different result from the tepid response Paul had experienced in Athens. What made the difference? The message: *Jesus Christ crucified.*

MY OWN TESTIMONY OF THE CROSS

I consider 1 Corinthians 1:18–25 my personal testimony because, as I mentioned, I spent seven years studying Greek philosophy—and modern philosophy—trying to find answers to life. One of the mind-sets that was fashionable in those days was called "linguistic philosophy" or, alternatively, "logical positivism." For two years at the University of Cambridge, I was a pupil of Ludwig Wittgenstein, who was known as the father of linguistic philosophy. He was a brilliant man—but definitely not a Christian. Therefore, I can deeply identify with these words of Paul:

> For the message of the cross is foolishness to those who are perishing, but to us who are being saved it is the power of God. For it is written: **"I will destroy the wisdom of the wise, and bring to nothing the understanding of the prudent."** Where is the wise? Where is the scribe? Where is the disputer of this age? Has not God made foolish the wisdom of this world? For since, in the wisdom of God, the world through wisdom did not know God, it pleased God through the foolishness of the message preached to save those who believe. For Jews request a sign, and Greeks seek after wisdom; but we preach Christ crucified, to the Jews a stumbling block and to the Greeks foolishness, but to those who are called, both Jews and Greeks, Christ the power of God and the wisdom of God. Because the foolishness of God is wiser than men, and the weakness of God is stronger than men.
>
> (1 Corinthians 1:18–25)

That is my testimony. In the providence of God, I never came to know God through human wisdom. Yet when I heard the foolishness of the cross preached, I responded to it and was saved. I was a Cambridge scholar who went to a Pentecostal church and heard a taxi driver preach. In the middle of his message, he was standing on a bench to demonstrate a point, and the bench collapsed, dropping him to the platform with a thud. If you could go much further in foolishness, I do not know where you would go! But his message was the lever that opened my heart to the message of salvation.

THE MEANING OF THE CROSS

For the sake of clarity, as we continue through this book, I need to explain exactly what I mean by "the cross." For many people from a variety of backgrounds, the cross is simply a symbol they hang around their necks or put on the walls of their churches or homes. I am not critical of those practices. In fact, when I have been in a strongly anti-Christian social environment, I have always been glad to see somebody with a cross around their neck, because it makes a bold statement in that environment.

However, when I talk about the cross, I am not speaking about a symbol. Neither am I merely speaking about an ancient means of execution. "The cross," as I will be using it, refers to *Jesus' sacrificial death on the cross and all that His death accomplished for us*. Rather than using all those phrases, I am simply condensing them to "the cross."

The New Testament presents us with a number of different reasons why nothing must ever be allowed to take the place of the cross. The Bible clearly tells us why we need the cross at the center—in the church in general, and in our own lives in particular. In the chapters that follow, we will consider six compelling reasons why we must keep the cross central in the church and in our lives.

CHAPTER 2

ONE ALL-SUFFICIENT
SACRIFICE

A COMPLETE SACRIFICE

The first aspect of the cross that we must keep central is that it represents *one perfect, all-sufficient sacrifice*. To begin our study of this aspect, we will examine a passage in Hebrews 10 that contrasts the priests of the old covenant with Jesus as the High Priest of the new covenant. One of the most striking contrasts is expressed in two positions: the priests of the old covenant always stood—they never sat down. But the High Priest of the new covenant, after He offered one sacrifice forever, sat down at the right hand of God.

The Old Testament priests remained standing because their task was never complete. However, Jesus sat down because His task was totally complete—He would never have to do it again. Let's read how the book of Hebrews describes this important principle:

And every priest stands ministering daily and offering repeatedly the same sacrifices, which can never take away

sins. But this Man, after He had offered one sacrifice for
sins forever, sat down at the right hand of God, from that
time waiting till His enemies are made His footstool. For
by one offering He has perfected forever those who are
being sanctified.   (Hebrews 10:11–14)

This passage expresses in the strongest possible linguistic forms the completeness of what Jesus did. By one sacrifice *"He has perfected."* The Greek verb is in the perfect tense, which means *to do something perfectly.* It is done; it is finished—never having to be done again or repeated. This complete sacrifice covers all time and all eternity.

The writer of Hebrews says of Jesus, *"But this Man, after He had offered one sacrifice for sins forever, sat down at the right hand of God"* (Hebrews 10:12). Again, Jesus sat down because He was never going to have to offer another sacrifice. By one sacrifice, He had made total and perfect provision for every need of every human being.

A PROPHETIC PREVIEW

The nature of the sacrifice Jesus made was prophetically described by the prophet Isaiah seven hundred years before it took place. Chapter 53 of the book of Isaiah is a great preview of the atonement of Jesus. Although Jesus is not named, He is the only one who answers this description. We begin with Isaiah 53:6:

All we like sheep have gone astray; we have turned every
one to his own way; and the LORD has laid on Him
[Jesus] the iniquity of us all.

Isaiah clearly states the problem of the whole human race—the one failing we all have in common. We may be European, American, Asian, or African, but this statement applies to every one of us: *"All we like sheep have gone astray; we have turned every one to his own way."* We have all turned our backs on God and His requirements and have gone our own way.

The Bible calls this *"iniquity,"* which is a very strong word. The best modern translation for iniquity would be "rebellion." The literal Hebrew expresses that God has "made to meet" on Jesus the iniquity, or rebellion, of the whole human race.

"Iniquity" also refers to the evil consequences of, and the punishment for, rebellion. Jesus' sacrifice is perfect because God visited upon Him the rebellion of all of us, along with all the evil consequences and judgment that were due to us because of that rebellion. In very simple language, all the evil due to us by justice came upon Jesus, so that all the good due to the sinless obedience of the Son of God might be made available to us. Jesus did it all by that one sacrifice.

In Isaiah 53:10, the prophet takes this picture one step further:

> *Yet it pleased the LORD to bruise* ["crush," various translations] *Him; He has put Him to grief; when You make His soul an offering for sin, He shall see His seed, He shall prolong His days, and the pleasure of the LORD shall prosper in His hand.*

Here is not only a depiction of Jesus' sacrifice but also a clear prediction of His resurrection. Verses 8–9 describe how *"He was cut off from the land of the living."* In other words, His life was taken from Him. So when the prophet says, *"He shall see His seed, He shall prolong his days,"* these realities could not take place without His resurrection.

Isaiah 53:10 says that God made the *"soul"* of Jesus the sin offering, or the guilt offering, for the entire human race. The magnitude of this principle is something our finite human minds cannot really comprehend. I believe that when Jesus was on the cross, our sicknesses and our pains were visited upon His *body*, but our sin came upon His *soul*. His perfectly righteous, holy soul was made sin with our sinfulness. Therefore, by that sacrifice He carried away our sin when He died.

THE ONLY REMEDY FOR SIN

The entire Bible has one consistent message: *there is only one remedy for sin—a sacrifice.* Every sacrifice of the Old Testament looks forward prophetically to the sacrifice of Jesus on the cross. It is important to understand the epistle to the Hebrews in this context. In Hebrews 10:3–4, the writer states,

> But in those sacrifices there is a reminder of sins every year. For it is not possible that the blood of bulls and goats could take away sins.

In the Old Testament, when the sacrifices were made every year, it was a reminder of the sins that had been committed.

Furthermore, those sacrifices could not take away sins. By way of example, the chief sacrifice of Israel was the sacrifice of the Day of Atonement. Yet it was valid only for one year—and it could not take away sin. It merely covered it. The atonement covered sin for the year until the sacrifice was due again. In that sense, it was a reminder of sin. Every year, the Jewish people were reminded that they had to deal with the sin issue; and they could deal with it only for one year.

However, the writer of Hebrews says of Jesus, *"But now, once at the end of the ages, He has appeared to put away sin by the sacrifice of Himself"* (Hebrews 9:26). Consequently, no more sacrifice is needed for sin. Paul essentially interprets this in 2 Corinthians 5:21 when he writes, *"For God made Him who knew no sin to be sin for us, that we might become the righteousness of God in Him."*

Many people who read this verse in 2 Corinthians do not realize that Paul had in mind the Old Testament sacrifices. We understand this context only when we realize that, according to the law of the Old Testament sacrifices, the animal sacrificed was identified with the sin of the person who sacrificed it. Therefore, when Jesus was sacrificed on the cross, He was identified with our sin.

This is a very simple but very profound exchange. God made Jesus to be sin with our sinfulness so that, in return, we might be made righteous with His righteousness. This is God's remedy for sin—there is no other.

I want to provide here a confession of this exchange, which is good to make on a regular basis. If you are a believer in the

Bible and in Jesus, then whether you have ever realized it or not, these words are true of you:

> God made Jesus to be sin with my sinfulness so that I might be made righteous with His righteousness.

I would encourage you to declare this confession out loud on a frequent basis.

"ALL THINGS" ARE PROVIDED

In Romans 8:31–32, Paul emphasizes the all-sufficiency of the sacrifice of Jesus:

> *What then shall we say to these things? If God is for us, who can be against us? He who did not spare His own Son, but delivered Him up for us all, how shall He not with Him also freely give us all things?*

"*All things*" are provided for us through the sacrifice of Jesus. God the Father, having given Jesus, will not withhold anything from us, but "*with Him also freely give[s] us all things.*" The one sacrifice of Jesus releases the total abundance of God's mercy and provision. We need no other basis—because there is no other basis. It is very important to understand this—because if you come to God for mercy and grace on any other basis except the sacrifice of Jesus on the cross, God will not meet you. Any premise other than Jesus' sacrifice for us is a false basis.

You and I cannot come to God on the basis of our good works, our religiosity, our family background, our morality, or our good intentions, because God is not impressed by any of these. They will not release the mercy and grace of God. The only catalyst that releases God's mercy and grace is the fact that Jesus was made sin with our sinfulness, died in our place, and rose again from the dead.

I urge you never to pass a day without meditating on this eternal truth. Never displace this truth from the center of your thoughts, your words, and your life. As soon as the cross becomes displaced, you will find that you are no longer enjoying the abundance of God's grace. You will find yourself struggling, perplexed, and confused. Very often, you will find yourself feeling guilty and not understanding what has happened. The reason behind all those experiences is that the cross has been displaced from the center of your life.

FROM LEGAL TO EXPERIENTIAL

The writer of Hebrews tells us, *"For by one offering* [Jesus] *has perfected forever those who are being sanctified"* (Hebrews 10:14). Now we come to the human element: *"those who are being sanctified."* Here the tense changes. What Jesus has done is perfect—but our appropriation of it is progressive. It is so important for us to understand this. Legally, we inherited everything when we were born again. We became a child of God, an heir of God and a co-heir with Jesus Christ. The entire inheritance is legally ours.

But, experientially, we do not yet possess it all. If you and I are honest with ourselves, we will recognize that none of us has yet appropriated all that Jesus has done for us on the cross. We *are being* sanctified. There is a process going on in us, the result of which is that all Jesus has done on the cross is being worked into our lives.

We could express the Christian life in this way: *the transition from the legal to the experiential.* Again, when we were born again, our inheritance in Christ legally became ours. But, experientially, we must make it our own. John 1:12 says this about the new birth: *"As many as received Him* [Jesus], *to them He gave the right* [Greek, "authority"] *to become children of God."*

In the new birth, we received authority to "become." The process by which we become is described in Hebrews 10:14 as *"being sanctified."* However, authority means nothing unless we *use* it. How much have we become, and how much do we have yet to become?

Remember, by one sacrifice, Jesus has made total and perfect provision for every need of every human being. His is the all-sufficient sacrifice.

As we conclude this chapter, would you like to acknowledge this amazing sacrifice for yourself? Let's do so together with the following prayer:

Lord Jesus, I declare that God made You to be sin with my sinfulness so that I might be made righteous with Your righteousness. Thank You that I am able to enter into this amazing exchange. I receive the inheritance that is legally mine by Your all-sufficient sacrifice. On the basis of what You did for me on the cross, I now come for mercy and grace to possess and walk in what You have provided. Amen.

CHAPTER 3

RELEASE OF
SUPERNATURAL GRACE

The second reason we must keep the cross at the center is that the cross releases God's supernatural grace into our lives. Christianity is not a set of rules. I remember one occasion when I was speaking to quite a large audience, and I said, somewhat casually, "Of course, Christianity is not a set of rules." That audience looked at me in astonishment. I think they might have been less shocked if I had said, "*There is no God.*"

It has become obvious to me over the years that Christianity is not a set of rules or laws. We will see how this contrasts with the law in the Old Testament. By the first century AD, Israel had been operating for fourteen hundred years under a set of laws given by God through Moses. And Paul tells us in Romans 7:12 that the law of Moses was perfect, righteous, holy, and good. When it comes to laws, we can never improve on the law of Moses. However, if the law of Moses could have provided a means of righteousness, there would have been no need for Jesus to come.

It seems to me that Christians who talk the most about grace sometimes know the least about it. There are people who say we are not under law. But then they construct their own set of religious rules, which is sometimes quite complicated. If the law of Moses could not bring righteousness, then neither can Baptist, Pentecostal, or Catholic law.

THE HUMAN PROBLEM

So we can never improve upon the law of Moses. However, the law of Moses failed. Why? Not because there was anything wrong with the law—but because there is a problem with the fleshly, or carnal, nature. We are unable to keep any law due to the weakness of our human nature. Paul says this very clearly in Galatians 3:11–12:

> But that no one is justified by the law in the sight of God is evident, for "the just shall live by faith." Yet the law is not of faith, but "the man who does them shall live by them."

Paul says no one can ever achieve righteousness with God by law. In the version of the Bible quoted above, the translators have inserted the word "the" before law. Actually, the Greek reads: "No one is justified by law." Using "the" is legitimate, because Paul primarily has in mind the law of Moses. But if you leave out the word "the," it is still true. No one can achieve righteousness with God by keeping any law, and there is no law that can enable us to achieve such righteousness.

That we are not justified by keeping laws is one of the statements most frequently made in the New Testament. It is also the statement that is the most persistently ignored by Christians. There must be at least a dozen places where the New Testament says—in one way or another—that we can never achieve righteousness with God by keeping a set of rules. Yet the majority of Christians somehow have the idea that if they keep the right rules, they will be all right with God. Clearly, this does not work—because God does not accept righteousness produced through our own efforts.

In truth, trying to keep laws tends to produce the exact opposite of freedom or righteousness. Those who focus on keeping laws become what is called "legalistic." When people become legalistic, they begin to believe that whatever section of the church they belong to is absolutely right. They say, "Our laws are right, and we're righteous because we keep them; others who don't keep our laws are not as righteous." Legalism tends to split up the church into a lot of different groups according to the particular set of laws each group is keeping.

ENTER THE CROSS

Since we cannot become righteous through law, what is the purpose of the cross? And how can we avail ourselves of its power for our lives?

One purpose of the cross is to bring us to the end of all our wisdom and righteousness. The cross is the supreme lesson that our own power is totally inadequate. This is something that is very easy to say but is not always easy to practice in our daily lives. The truth is, we can begin to enter into the grace of God only when we have come to the end of ourselves.

As you read this book, you are no doubt thinking about some of the problems and pressures you are facing in life. Sometimes our reaction to our problems is to ask, "What are You doing, God?" Here is the answer: God is gently but firmly bringing you to the end of yourself, to the end of all your own best efforts. He is helping you to recognize that the best you can do does not even begin to be good enough. Why? Because the Lord wants to provide a release in your life that is totally from Him—something that *is* good enough to get the job done.

THE CROSS IS STRONGER

Let us return to a passage that we looked at in chapter 1 of this book, where Paul is clear on this issue:

> *For Jews request a sign, and Greeks seek after wisdom; but we preach Christ crucified, to the Jews a stumbling block and to the Greeks foolishness, but to those who are called, both Jews and Greeks, Christ the power of God and the wisdom of God. Because the foolishness of God is wiser than men, and the weakness of God is stronger than men.*
> (1 Corinthians 1:22–25)

When he was in Corinth, Paul preached Christ crucified. It is easy to preach Christ as the great Teacher or as the wonderful Healer. But that message alone does not get the job done. We must preach Christ *crucified*. We find Christ as the power of God and the wisdom of God only when we have come to the end of our own power and our own wisdom. Paul's conclusion is summed up in one marvelous statement: *"The foolishness of God is wiser than men, and the weakness of God is stronger than men."*

In one word, the foolishness of God and the weakness of God is the *cross*. The cross is the ultimate in weakness. We cannot imagine anything weaker than a man dying in agony on a cross, breathing his last. Also, it is totally foolish that God should send into the world His Son, the one perfect Man, and then allow Him to die a criminal's death. Thus, the cross is totally weak and totally foolish.

In our lives, when we come to the end of all our cleverness, wisdom, strength, and righteousness, we then make a wonderful discovery. What is it? We find that the cross is stronger than man's strength and wiser than man's wisdom. Again, with my background in Greek philosophy, I find these words totally true.

In the cross, God's weakness is stronger than our strength. In the cross, God's foolishness is wiser than our wisdom. Here is the problem: it is hard for most of us to let go of our own strength and our own wisdom. Most of us want God's wisdom and strength. But we still want to hold on to our own wisdom and strength as well. We want to cling to them as if they really have some eternal value.

The truth is that God does not deal with us on that basis. We *must* come to the end of our own wisdom and strength before God will release His grace into our lives.

PAUL'S "THORN IN THE FLESH"

Paul makes some amazing statements along this theme. In 2 Corinthians 12:7, he writes from personal experience,

Lest I should be exalted above measure by the abundance of the revelations, a thorn in the flesh was given to me, a messenger [or angel] of Satan to buffet me [to keep beating me], lest I be exalted above measure.

Paul is referring to the revelations God gave him. When people receive revelations, they can easily fall into pride (in the sense of haughtiness or arrogance) if they are not careful. But God loved Paul so much that He helped him guard against pride in a very unusual way. The way I see it, He released an "angel of Satan" to follow Paul around from place to place. That agent would stir up trouble and persecution, thus keeping Paul humble.

Most of us would say we want to be humble. However, we may be surprised at the means God will use to answer that request! See again what Paul says:

Lest I should be exalted above measure by the abundance of the revelation, a thorn in the flesh was given me, a messenger [angel] of Satan to buffet me [to keep beating me], lest I be exalted above measure.

The phrase *"a thorn in the flesh"* is a metaphor taken from the Old Testament. It refers to Joshua's warning to the children of Israel to eliminate the Canaanites who occupied the land. He told the Israelites that if they allowed the Canaanites to coexist with them, they would become *"scourges on your sides and thorns in your eyes"* (Joshua 23:13). Many of us have "thorns in our flesh" of our own making. Why? Because we have come into the promised land, yet we have allowed a number of "Canaanites" to hang around.

In Paul's case, however, the thorn was not something for which Paul himself was responsible. It was something God did in his life. If we study Paul's career, he was unlike any of the other apostles. They all were persecuted and had troubles, but Paul's troubles were in a category by themselves. There was hardly a city he visited where a riot did not start.

The most ridiculous factors would provoke a riot. In Philippi, all Paul did was cast a demon out of a fortune-telling slave girl. Suddenly, the whole city was in an uproar. Within a few hours, Paul and his colleague Silas were in the maximum-security jail. That is simply not logical. It cannot be explained by any process of reasoning. There was a satanic angel stirring things up against him. Basically, wherever Paul went, trouble got stirred up; wherever he went, there was usually a riot or a revival—or both!

SUFFICIENT GRACE

Writing about this constant presence that brought harassment, Paul then says, *"Concerning this thing I pleaded with the Lord three times that it might depart from me"* (2 Corinthians 12:8). However, God would not remove this thorn. Sometimes, when we say God does not answer our prayers, we must remember that no is also an answer. God's answer to Paul was,

"My grace is sufficient for you, for My strength is made perfect in weakness" (2 Corinthians 12:9). How true this is.

When we operate by our own strength, there is no way for us to identify God's strength. Neither we nor anyone else can see God's strength—because it is hidden by our strength and wisdom. But when we have come to the end of our own strength, then we find we have new strength. At that point, we know this strength is from God. God's strength is made perfect in our weakness. That is why Paul could say the following:

> *Therefore most gladly I will rather boast in my infirmities* [weaknesses], *that the power of Christ may rest upon me. Therefore I take pleasure in infirmities, in reproaches, in needs, in persecutions, in distresses, for Christ's sake. For when I am weak, then I am strong.*
>
> (2 Corinthians 12:9–10)

I believe in making confessions based on the Word of God—but Paul's confession to take pleasure in infirmities is one I would never ask anyone to make. It took me years to come to the place where I was willing to make it myself. I have come to the point where—on my good days—I am prepared to make this confession. But I would not ask anybody to make this confession unless they were led by the Holy Spirit because, once they have declared it, they have committed themselves to it.

You may want to think ahead before you make such a confession. Would you be willing to *take pleasure in*—not merely tolerate, not merely endure, not merely suffer with grace—infirmities, weaknesses, distresses, persecution, and needs?

Why would Paul want to take pleasure in weakness? Because he had learned this secret: *When we come to the end of our own strength, wisdom, and resources, then God releases His grace.*

I have grown to appreciate this little saying: "Grace begins where human ability ends." We do not qualify for the grace of God as long as we can do something for ourselves. Why should God release His grace when we are operating in our own strength? But when we have come to the place where we cannot do something, and yet it has to be done, then we qualify for the release of God's grace.

THE FAITH OF GOD'S SON

In Galatians 2:20, we find another of Paul's confessions. It is interesting to notice how many times Paul confessed his faith and his stand. In the New Testament, you will never find any of the apostles making any negative confessions. However, when you observe contemporary Christianity, including some of its ministers, you will hear an abundance of negative confessions: "I can't do this," "I don't feel like this," "I wish I could," "I couldn't," and so on.

That is not the way the apostles talked—not because they were self-confident, but because they had come to the end of their own strength. Thus, Paul makes this confession:

I am crucified with Christ: nevertheless I live; yet not I,
but Christ liveth in me: and the life which I now live in the
flesh I live by the faith of the Son of God, who loved me,
and gave Himself for me.   (Galatians 2:20 KJV)

Please note that, for this verse, I switched from the *New King James Version*, which I am using primarily in this book, to the old King James, which contains the literal translation of an important phrase. The *New King James* translates the phrase as *"...by faith in the Son of God."* But the King James says, *"...by the faith of the Son of God."* It is not my faith I am relying upon. When Jesus came to indwell me, He came in with His faith.

In Paul's confession here in Galatians 2:20, he asserts that as a result of the sacrifice of Christ on the cross, he had come to the end of his own life. When Paul came to the cross, he died. Now it is not Paul who is living, but Christ who is living in him.

I would challenge you to make this your own personal confession:

I am crucified with Christ; nevertheless I live; yet not
I, but Christ lives in me; and the life I now live in the
flesh I live by the faith of the Son of God, who loved
me and gave Himself for me.

THE KEY TO HOLINESS

I believe that understanding Paul's declaration is the key to New Testament holiness—*"without which,"* the Bible says, *"no one will see the Lord"* (Hebrews 12:14). In Leviticus 11:45, God declares, *"You shall therefore be holy, for I am holy."* In the Old Testament, holiness consisted in keeping a set of very complicated rules.

In the New Testament, while writing to believers about holiness, Peter quotes this passage from Leviticus: *"Be holy, for I am holy"* (1 Peter 1:16). However, it is important for us to realize that there is a total difference between Old Testament and New Testament holiness. Old Testament holiness was based on keeping the Mosaic law. In contrast, New Testament holiness is not based on keeping a set of rules; but Christ enables us to fulfill the law in Him. New Testament holiness is achieved by dying to self and letting Christ live out His life through you.

Therefore, it is not my holiness, but Christ's. I like to express it like this: "It is not struggling but yielding; it is not effort but union—union with Christ."

There was once a godly lady who was admired for her holy life. One day, another Christian said to her, "Sister, how do you deal with temptation?" She quickly replied, "When the devil knocks at the door, I just let Jesus answer."

Her statement sums it up in a nutshell: *"not I, but Christ."* Living a victorious life in Christ does not come by what I can do—my best effort, or flexing my spiritual muscle. It comes from yielding. I live by letting Christ do His work in me, through me, and for me.

PRUNED FOR FRUITFULNESS

In John 15, we see another picture of Jesus living His life through us. In that chapter, Jesus uses the example of the vine and the branches to perfectly illustrate this life:

> *I am the true vine, and My Father is the vinedresser.*
>
> (John 15:1)

> *Abide in Me, and I in you. As the branch cannot bear fruit of itself, unless it abides in the vine, neither can you, unless you abide in Me. I am the vine, you are the branches. He who abides in Me, and I in him, bears much fruit; for without Me you can do nothing.*
>
> (John 15:4–5)

Please notice that *the Father* is the vinedresser. Be careful about letting other people prune you. The Father is the only one who has the skill and the sensitivity to do the pruning. There are some churches and fellowships where the leaders want to do the pruning—and they want to prune everyone.

Use caution about submitting to human pruning. Not only will it be needlessly painful, but those doing the pruning may also cut off the wrong branch. The business of ministers and leaders of God's people is not to do the pruning. It is to help people submit to God's pruning and to share in that process with them.

There is much we can learn from Jesus' picture of the vine and the branches. Have you ever seen a branch of a vine really struggling to bring forth fruit? It does not happen through any effort of the branch; fruit comes because the life of the vine is flowing into the branch.

This little parable includes all three persons of the Godhead. The Father is the vinedresser, Jesus is the vine, and the Holy Spirit is the sap. We, of course, are those branches. As the Holy Spirit flows through the vine into the branches, the branches bring forth the fruit of the Spirit.

The very word "*fruit*" tells us that results do not come by our efforts. No tree has ever brought forth fruit by exerting effort. Similarly, no Christian can bring forth fruit by effort. We must come to the place where we cease from our struggling—and, in a certain sense, cease from all our good works. It is not just our sins that must come to an end. It is also every human effort we think we can do for God. All of these efforts must come to an end and yield to Jesus.

When we have yielded everything to Jesus, then we can say with Paul, "*I can do all things through Christ who strengthens me*" (Philippians 4:13). A more literal reading of the Greek text of this verse would be, "I can do all things through the One who empowers me within."

OUR LOVING HEAVENLY FATHER

You can keep all the rules, follow all the principles, and listen to all the teaching. However, you will never know real victory unless the grace of God is released through the cross. In fact, if we do not know how to release the grace of God, rules won't help us. The more rules we try to keep, the worse our problems will become.

In the end, if rules are your chosen method, you are likely to throw all the rules and principles overboard and cry, "It's no good, I just can't do it!" And you would be perfectly correct. There is only one Person who can fulfill God's law perfectly, and His name is Jesus. When He is allowed to live His life in us, and when we have submitted to the cross by coming to the end of ourselves—then He is abundantly able to give us victory. None of us can truly walk in the Spirit apart from the grace released through the cross.

The beautiful fact about grace is that if we do not do things perfectly right, the Lord does not reject us. He patiently shows us where we went wrong and encourages us to try again. I have been a Christian since I was a young man. When I think of all the mistakes I have made and all the ways I have gone wrong, I am amazed that God still keeps His hand on me.

If you find yourself struggling as a Christian, never despair. The Lord may deal with you severely. He may correct you. He may do things in your life that you cannot understand. However, He will never give up on you. You may have bitter memories of your childhood and of parents who did not understand you or were not always loving. But please bear in mind that you have another Father who is God. He is very patient, very understanding, and very gentle.

Would you like to confirm the truths we have learned in this chapter with a prayer and a declaration?

Lord Jesus, the cross upon which You suffered and died is stronger and more powerful than any rules or any law I could follow. The cross releases me from those rules, and opens the way for Your supernatural grace. Lord, please live Your life in me. Let the sap of the Holy Spirit flow within me, producing fruit in my life that would be impossible apart from You. Thank You, Lord, for a supernatural release of grace in my life through the cross. Amen.

CHAPTER 4

RELEASE OF SUPERNATURAL CONFIRMATION

The third reason we need to keep the cross at the center is that the supernatural confirmation of God is released when we preach the message of the cross. Let us refer again to 1 Corinthians 2:4–5, where Paul writes:

> And my speech and my preaching were not with persuasive words of human wisdom, but in demonstration of the Spirit and of power, that your faith should not be in the wisdom of men but in the power of God.

Later, in 2 Corinthians 10:10, Paul quotes his critics, who said his bodily presence was weak and his speech was contemptible. Paul must not have been a great orator or an especially impressive person. Tradition holds that he was rather short, with bowed legs—a very unimposing figure. However, Paul did not rely on his eloquence or his wisdom. He relied on one characteristic above all others: *the supernatural confirmation of the Holy Spirit to the message that he preached.*

THE FULL GOSPEL

It is important to notice from the above passage that the reality of the Holy Spirit can be demonstrated. He Himself is invisible—but He is demonstrated by what He does. We cannot see the Holy Spirit. But we can see the signs and the miracles He performs. These are God's own attestation of the message preached.

Because of my study of philosophy, I especially appreciate the above passage. The philosophy I studied was very fashionable fifty years ago, but today it is quite out of date. If I had built my life on that wisdom, I would have a crumbling foundation underneath me now. However, when I met Jesus, I had an experience of the supernatural power of God. That reality has been an unshakeable foundation throughout my life.

Paul writes in Romans 15:18–19:

For I will not dare to speak of any of those things which Christ has not accomplished through me, in word and deed, to make the Gentiles obedient—in mighty signs and wonders, by the power of the Spirit of God, so that from Jerusalem and round about to Illyricum I have fully preached the gospel of Christ.

Paul is saying here, in so many words, that he is only interested in what Christ has done through him and not in what he has done on his own. Paul believed that without the signs and wonders, he had not fully preached the gospel. He knew that the supernatural confirmation of God would be released as he preached the message of the cross.

HEART OBEDIENCE

In the late 1950s, I was the principal of a college established to train teachers in Kenya, East Africa. At that time, the Africans were striving for education. As a result, they were willing to go to a college, obey all its rules, and do everything they were instructed to do. If we told them to be baptized, they would be baptized. If we told them to sing hymns, they would sing hymns. Why? Because their future depended on it. However, after my first wife, Lydia, and I had been there about a year, I realized that most of what they did was external conformity for the sake of their education. There was very little real heart obedience.

Out of this concern, I took the step to summon the entire student body of about one hundred twenty students. When they had all gathered together, I said to them something like this: "I want to thank you for the way you cooperate with us and the way you do what we tell you to do. I realize you do it because your education depends on it. I'm grateful. But in the minds of most of you, there's a big unanswered question. And that unanswered question is this: 'Is the Bible really a message from God, or is it just a white man's book that doesn't apply to Africans?'"

They were a bit taken aback, because that was exactly what they were thinking. Then I told them something else that shocked them: "What's more, I can't answer that question. There's only one way you can find out the answer for yourself. That will come only if you have an experience of the supernatural power of God in your life. Then you'll know it didn't come from America and it didn't come from Britain. It came from heaven."

In the ensuing months, I put the Word of God before them in every way I could, because it had the authority to change them. Afterward, I went away and prayed for about six months. What was the result? God began to pour out His Spirit on those students. We could not get them to sleep at night in the dormitories because they were so busy praying! In the next six months, we had all nine gifts of the Holy Spirit in operation among those young Africans. Their lives were radically changed when they experienced God's supernatural power—the confirmation of the message of the cross.

During that period, we saw two of the students raised from the dead. One was a young man and the other was a young woman. The young woman, whose name was Teresa, became extremely sick and went home to her village. A few days later, Teresa's brother came to us on a bicycle and told us that she was dying.

Lydia and I put the bicycle on the roof of our car and set out with the brother. After a long journey, we arrived at the village where Teresa was in a little clinic. She had apparently died before we were able to get there. All the family members were outside moaning and weeping—it was like a scene from the New Testament. Lydia and I walked into the room where Teresa was, having no plans about what to do. We just knelt down on either side of the bed and prayed. After quite some time, Teresa sat up and said, "Has anyone got a Bible?"

I said, "Yes, I do."

She said, "Read Psalm 41."

So I read Psalm 41. We did not know why she had asked to have that psalm read. Then Teresa explained that when she died, her spirit left her body and went to a place full of beautiful, bright lights. There was a man in that place reading Psalm 41 in the Bible. So she had wanted to know what was in Psalm 41!

Believe me, an experience of the supernatural power of God creates obedience from the heart. When we present the message of the cross and of the kingdom of God, it brings the supernatural confirmation of the Holy Spirit. When that confirmation comes, hearts are changed.

Are you longing for the release of such supernatural confirmation? Why not tell the Lord about your desire using the following prayer?

Lord, I long for more than my own speech—more than my own persuasive words and my own human wisdom. I want to see a demonstration of the Spirit and of Your power—coming as a release of the supernatural confirmation of God when the message of the cross is preached. Lord, please bring this supernatural release into my life in a greater way today. Amen.

CHAPTER 5

THE SOLE BASIS FOR
SATAN'S DEFEAT

VICTORY THROUGH THE CROSS

Here is the fourth reason the cross must be at the center of all that we believe and do: the cross is the sole basis for the total defeat of Satan. This truth is extremely important—and it is a truth our enemy wishes we never would have discovered. Furthermore, he will do everything in his power to prevent us from apprehending, understanding, or applying it.

Through the cross, Jesus Christ administered to Satan a total, permanent, and irrevocable defeat. Satan cannot change this eternal truth. Moreover, he realized his defeat too late. When he procured the death of Jesus on the cross, he thought he had won. But to the contrary, he had actually procured his own defeat. Thus, since his demise at the cross, the enemy has been doing everything in his power to obscure this truth and to hide it from the eyes of the church.

If you want to resist and oppose Satan in your own life or in any situation, you cannot do it on any basis other than Jesus' victory over him through the cross. If you challenge him on any other basis, you will be defeated. Why? Because the enemy of our souls is much stronger and much cleverer than we are in our own strength and wisdom.

When the Lord led me into the ministry of deliverance from evil spirits, I soon discovered that demons are not impressed by our theology or our church denominations. They could not care less if you are an evangelical, a charismatic, or a Catholic. However, when you deal with demons on the basis of what Jesus accomplished on the cross, that is when they *"believe—and tremble"* (James 2:19). I have witnessed demons trembling when confronted with the reality of the defeat that Satan suffered through the cross.

A TOTAL VICTORY

To understand how Jesus gained victory over Satan, let us first read Jesus' statement in Luke 11:21–22:

> *When a strong man, fully armed, guards his own palace, his goods are in peace. But when a stronger than he comes upon him and overcomes him, he takes from him all his armor in which he trusted, and divides his spoils.*

The picture here is of a tyrant, an oppressor. He resides confidently in a very strong castle in which he is total master. In this castle, he has amassed a great deal of ill-gotten spoil and plunder from those he has oppressed. He also has under his control a multitude of slaves whom he forces to do his will.

He sits in his stronghold fully armed, thinking he is undefeatable. However, a second man who is stronger comes against him and defeats him. Please notice that the stronger man takes from the first man all of his weapons, releases his captives, and plunders his goods.

In this parable, the first strong man is Satan. The second strong man is Jesus. Satan had everything under his control in his stronghold. He had enslaved humanity. He had robbed us of all the wealth and blessings that God our Father intended us to have. Satan was sitting there thinking he was undefeatable. Then along came Jesus. For that, we have good reason to praise and thank the Lord!

On the cross, the Lord Jesus, without any military weapons, administered to Satan a total, permanent, and irrevocable defeat. Then, having defeated the enemy, Jesus took from him all his weapons and said to his captives, "Now you can go free! And while you're going, help yourself to some of the spoil."

This parable therefore represents Jesus' own picture of what He would achieve by His death on the cross.

In Colossians 2:13–15, we read what was accomplished for us when Jesus defeated Satan:

> *And you, being dead in your trespasses and the uncircumcision of your flesh, He* [God the Father] *has made alive together with Him* [Jesus Christ the Son], *having forgiven you all trespasses, having wiped out the handwriting of requirements that was against us, which was contrary to us. And He has taken it out of the way, having nailed it to the cross. Having disarmed principalities and*

powers, He made a public spectacle of them, triumphing
over them in it.

Paul says here that Jesus *"disarmed principalities and*
powers." These principalities and powers are Satan's legions.
These are the same principalities and powers referenced by
Paul in Ephesians 6:12:

For we do not wrestle against flesh and blood, but against
principalities, against powers, against the rulers of the
darkness of this age, against spiritual hosts of wickedness
in the heavenly places.

After Jesus defeated the legions of Satan and stripped
them of their weapons, He proceeded to make an open show
of them. We need to understand the basis on which He did
that, because we can believe it in theory yet not necessarily
apply it in our lives.

DEALING WITH THE DEVIL

Satan's greatest weapon against humanity is guilt.
Thankfully, Jesus' victory over guilt was complete—accomplished by His work on the cross. Here is a simple picture,
from my own imagination, of what could have happened many
ages ago in Satan's quest to ruin humanity.

First, we know that Satan, at least in the time of Job, had
access to the presence of God. How do we know this? Because
Scripture tells us that when the angels came to present themselves before the Lord, Satan joined the throng. (See Job 1:6–
7.) It was typical of him because his attitude was, "Well, God,

I know I made a mistake. But here I am. I'm still coming to Your presence."

According to my understanding, the only person who spotted Satan was the Lord, because Paul says the devil can disguise himself as an angel of light. (See 2 Corinthians 11:14.) Once his presence had been uncovered, God and Satan had a discussion about Job. (I have always been rather glad I was not the person about whom they had that discussion!)

I picture Satan as an impudent, defiant braggart. With his big mouth, he says to the Lord, "Listen, God, I know You're a righteous, just, and holy God. I know I'm a rebel. I see that lake of fire, and I know that's where I'm headed. I know I deserve to go there, and I'm not arguing that point. However, I just want to tell You one thing: those human beings You made in Your image and likeness whom You love so much—I've convinced them to be rebels just like me. Therefore, remember this, when You send me to that lake of fire, Your justice demands that You send them along with me."

How should God respond to this challenge? I picture God not saying a word in response. (Sometimes the best way to deal with the devil is not to argue with him but to ignore him. That really upsets him.) God did not say anything, but He had a plan. His plan was Jesus.

Jesus came into the world as the last Adam. (See 1 Corinthians 15:45.) He totally identified with the Adamic race. Satan went after Him, eventually procuring His death. The enemy's thinking was that once the Messiah was dead, He would be unable to set up the kingdom of God. However, when Jesus died on the cross, He became the representative of the whole Adamic race. All our guilt was laid upon Him. He paid the total penalty. When He died and was buried, our guilt was banished forever. And by His death and resurrection, we can receive the kingdom of God within us. Our only obligation is to believe this by faith.

Accordingly, by the work of the cross, God has made a way for humanity to be reprieved from the lake of fire. In His justice, God can forgive us and punish Satan, because there is no suggestion anywhere in the Bible that Satan has any other destiny except the lake of fire.

Jesus did not take upon Himself the nature of angels. Therefore, He cannot be a substitute for angels. Jesus is the last Adam; thus, He was able to be the substitute for the whole Adamic race—and *only* for the Adamic race. Eternity will be too short to discover why God cared so much about humanity. But again, on the basis of what Jesus did, God can now justly punish Satan when it suits Him. And God can also justly acquit those who accept the sacrifice of Jesus on their behalf.

Deliverance from Guilt

Through the death of Jesus, God provided for two areas of forgiveness to deliver us from our guilt. One has to do with our past guilt; the other, with our future guilt. First, God made provision for the past. All our acts of disobedience were punished in Jesus. Paul states in Colossians 2:13 that God forgave us all our trespasses. Again, He can forgive us without compromising His justice—making our past clear.

If you are a true believer in Jesus and have accepted His provision, there is nothing from the past against you in the records of heaven. Every evil deed you have ever done has been blotted out. God has said He will remember them no more. (See Jeremiah 31:34.) He has cast these past sins into the sea. (See Micah 7:19.) As Corrie ten Boom used to say, God has put up a sign beside that sea that says "No Fishing!"

As believers in Jesus, we should have a confident assurance that all our past sins are totally forgiven, never to be remembered again. Of course, if we have committed sins that have not been confessed, that is not necessarily true. The remedy for us is to confess these sins, because *"if we confess our sins, [God] is faithful and just to forgive us our sins and to cleanse us from all unrighteousness"* (1 John 1:9).

However, God still had to make provision for the future, lest we go back and start sinning all over again. To make this provision, He removed the law of Moses as the requirement for achieving righteousness with Him. Paul says God nailed the law, with its commandments and ordinances, to the cross. (See Colossians 2:14.) Once we come to the cross and continue in its power, we are outside the territory of the law as a means of righteousness. (This is a topic we will be dealing with more fully in a later chapter.)

Righteousness by Faith Alone

But this issue of the removal of the law leaves us with a question: Since the law is no longer a requirement for righteousness, what *is* the requirement? The requirement for righteousness is now, simply, faith. We are counted righteous not by keeping a set of rules but by faith in Jesus Christ.

Paul uses Abraham as an example of such faith. Quoting from Genesis 15:6, he writes, *"Abraham believed God, and it was accounted to him for righteousness"* (Romans 4:3). Faith was accounted to Abraham for righteousness. Paul concludes in Romans 4:22–25:

> And therefore *"it was accounted to him* [Abraham] *for righteousness."* Now it was not written for his sake alone that it was imputed [accounted] to him, but also for us. It shall be imputed to us who believe in Him who raised up Jesus our Lord from the dead, who was delivered up because of our offenses, and was raised because of our justification.

Therefore, we are in the same category with Abraham if we believe the record of what Jesus accomplished on the cross. The Scripture says Jesus was delivered to death because of our offenses, and He was raised up from the dead for our justification, in order that righteousness might be imputed to us.

So again, just as it was with Abraham, righteousness is imputed to us on the basis of our faith. Abraham did not earn righteousness by keeping laws—it came through his faith. Likewise, righteousness is not imputed to us because of what we do—it comes to us because of *what we believe.*

Faith is the only basis for righteousness that is accepted by God. As I understand the gospel, God does not permit us to add anything whatsoever to that requirement of faith.

Righteousness is not imputed to us on the basis of faith plus something: not faith plus good works, faith plus the church, faith plus baptism, or faith plus good intentions.

The cry of the Reformation was "sola fide"—*by faith alone.* This was the great recovered truth of the Reformation. It is only by faith that we can be accounted righteous with God. Not only has He abolished the law of Moses as a requirement for achieving righteousness, but He has not substituted any other law. For this we should praise Him.

As I have taught this truth over the years, I have seen Christians with their mouths open, gaping at me in astonishment. By now, I am used to this response. But this is the central truth of the gospel, and it is astounding how many people say they believe the gospel and do not understand this basic fact.

Peace Through Christ

As we enter fully into freedom from guilt, we can defeat the enemy's great weapon against us. Let's examine one other Scripture. Speaking further about what Jesus did for us on the cross, Paul writes:

> *For He Himself is our peace, who has made both* [Jew and Gentile] *one, and has broken down the middle wall of separation, having abolished in His flesh the enmity, that is, the law of commandments contained in ordinances, so as to create in Himself one new man from the two, thus making peace, and that He might reconcile*

them both to God in one body through the cross, thereby
putting to death the enmity.   (Ephesians 2:14–16)

Through His death on the cross, Jesus abolished *"the law
of commandments contained in ordinances"* and thereby abolished the enmity that the law produces. Focusing on the
requirements of the law does not bring peace; it brings enmity
and separation.

First, it has brought enmity between Jew and non-Jew for
some thirty-five hundred years. The reality is that many Jews
who observe the law of Moses believe that keeping the law
makes them more righteous than those who do not observe
the law. However, many of those who do not keep the law
declare that they are just as good as the Jews are, and maybe
better. This is an obvious point of enmity between the two
groups.

Second, the law brings enmity between God and man.
When we come under the law and break it, we become enemies of God.

In light of this enmity, and in order for us to achieve righteousness, God had to set aside the requirements of the law of
Moses. Again, Paul refers to the law as *"the law of commandments contained in ordinances."* Holding on to the law is similar
to the state of mind of a person who has fallen overboard into
the ocean and is holding on to a plank for survival. That plank
represents the law—and we believe if we let go of the plank, we
are going to drown.

The truth of the matter is, we *must* let go and drown, because the plank will never save us. We drown by dying with Christ, receiving His sacrifice for us on the cross, and coming up again into new life. As Paul wrote:

> Do you not know that as many of us as were baptized into Christ Jesus were baptized into His death? Therefore we were buried with Him through baptism into death, that just as Christ was raised from the dead by the glory of the Father, even so we also should walk in newness of life.
>
> (Romans 6:3–4)

Continual Forgiveness

As we live the Christian life, we may have our problems, and we may have our defeats. But our faith is continually reckoned to us for righteousness. At the Last Supper, Jesus warned Peter that he would deny Him three times that night. Then He said to Peter: *"Simon, Simon! Indeed, Satan has asked for you, that he may sift you as wheat. But I have prayed for you, that your faith should not fail"* (Luke 22:31–32).

Jesus did not pray that Peter would not deny Him. He prayed that Peter's faith would not fail. It was as if Jesus was saying, "Peter, you're going to do a lot of bad things. But if you keep on believing, I'll see you through."

That is good news for all of us. If we can just keep believing, God will bring us through.

If we think of the story of Abraham, the father of our faith, we see that Abraham did quite a number of wrong things—even after righteousness had been reckoned to him. Twice, he let his wife be taken into a Gentile harem, which was not a good thing to do. (See Genesis 12:10–20; 20.)

I believe God did not approve of Abraham's decision. However, even while Abraham was making that decision and carrying it out, his faith was still being accounted to him for righteousness. If most believers could only grasp this amazing truth, they would heave a sigh of relief.

Of course, this does not mean God encourages us to do bad things. But if we are sincerely seeking to do what He wants, even if we make mistakes, our faith is still counted to us for righteousness. God's children should relax, understanding that they do not have to hold on to the law. They just need to keep believing in Jesus and what He did on the cross.

Freedom from Condemnation and Accusation

By the provision of the cross, God has enabled us to be free from guilt. Satan has nothing more that he can accuse us of. In Romans 5:1, we are told, *"Therefore, having been justified by faith, we have peace with God."* We have also been freed from the weight of condemnation, as it says in Romans 8:1: *"There is therefore now no condemnation to those who are in Christ Jesus."*

I see the first eight chapters of Romans as a spiritual journey—what I call the "Roman Pilgrimage." Chapter 8 is the pilgrimage's destination, which is the Spirit-controlled life. The culmination of this journey occurs as we fully enter into the reality of our eternal, inseparable union with Jesus Christ. (See Romans 8:35–39.)

Chapter 8 is the victory chapter. But verse one is the only doorway into this chapter: *"There is therefore now no condemnation...."* If you are under condemnation, you cannot live the Spirit-led life described in Romans 8. Most Christians come under feelings of condemnation again and again. As a result, they lose their freedom in the Holy Spirit. They cannot stay in the life of Romans 8 because they have not learned the basis of being free from condemnation.

There is a great difference between guilt and conviction of sin. Guilt is often vague and general, while conviction is specific. When the Holy Spirit convicts us of sin, He tells us exactly what we have done wrong and what is required of us to put it right. Often He shows us specifically how we need to repent—perhaps even involving confession to an injured party or restitution for our wrongdoing.

Guilt, on the other hand, is never resolved. When we feel guilty, we often have a vague sense that we have not done quite enough, that we do not measure up to the standard of a "good Christian" or that God is somehow displeased with us. Thus, as we have noted, guilt is Satan's greatest single weapon against humanity.

Revelation 12 describes Satan and his angels being cast out of heaven. Some people say the event pictured there has already happened, but I personally believe it is still in the future. In verse 10, we are given an excellent picture of how our enemy operates against us today.

Then I heard a loud voice saying in heaven, "Now salvation, and strength, and the kingdom of our God, and the power of His Christ have come, for the accuser of our brethren, who accused them before our God day and night, has been cast down.

The event of Satan's expulsion still being in the future, the above verse describes where Satan is and what he is doing at this present time. And what is he doing? *Satan is accusing us before God.* That is one explanation for why we may experience such dark, deep, moody feelings at times. An atmosphere of guilt and condemnation is being created around us that we must learn to deal with. Satan's purpose in accusing us is to try to prove that we are guilty.

We may wonder why God does not stop Satan's accusations. It is because the Lord has already given *us* the power to stop him. He will not do for us what we can do for ourselves. Verse 11 of Revelation 12 gives us a very clear answer as to how we can stop Satan's accusations and deal with our guilt: *"They overcame him [Satan] by the blood of the Lamb and by the word of their testimony."*

Please note that there is a direct conflict between God's people and Satan. Some people would like to tell us that Satan cannot cause problems for Christians. That idea is neither true nor scriptural.

Revelation 12:11 tells us that we overcome Satan when we testify personally to what the Word of God says the blood of Jesus does for us. That is our testimony.

Under the old covenant, the blood of the Passover lamb granted the Israelites immunity from judgment. At the first Passover, the children of Israel were required to sprinkle the blood of the lamb on the lintel and doorposts of their homes for protection from judgment and death. To sprinkle the blood, they used a bunch of an herb called hyssop. They dipped the hyssop into a basin containing the lamb's blood, sprinkled the blood, and were saved. (See Exodus 12:1–30.)

For us, the blood of Jesus has already been shed; Christ our Passover Lamb has been sacrificed for us. (See 1 Corinthians 5:7.) His blood is available to us, and we apply it by our testimony. To overcome Satan, we testify personally to what the Word of God says the blood of Jesus does for us. The following are two confessions, or proclamations, based entirely on the Word of God, that declare what the blood of Jesus and the cross accomplish for us.

CONFESSING THE POWER OF THE BLOOD

The first is a confession of what the blood of Jesus does for us, and includes footnoted scriptural references. I would encourage you to use this confession when you feel guilty, condemned, or under the oppressive cloud of accusation from the enemy. Speak it boldly in faith out loud—declaring Jesus' total victory on the cross over Satan.

Through the blood of Jesus, I am redeemed out of the hand of the devil.[1]

Through the blood of Jesus, all my sins are forgiven.[2]

Through the blood of Jesus, I am continually being cleansed from all sin.[3]

Through the blood of Jesus, I am justified, made righteous, just-as-if-I'd never sinned.[4]

Through the blood of Jesus, I am sanctified, made holy, set apart to God.[5]

Through the blood of Jesus, I have boldness to enter into the presence of God.[6]

Through the blood of Jesus, I overcome the work of Satan.[7]

The blood of Jesus cries out continually to God in heaven on my behalf.[8]

[1]Ephesians 1:7; 1 Peter 1:19. [2]Ephesians 1:7. [3]1 John 1:7. [4]Romans 5:9. [5]Hebrews 13:12. [6]Hebrews 10:19. [7]Revelation 12:11. [8]Hebrews 12:24.

CONFESSING THE TRUTHS OF REVELATION 12:11

The second confession is based on Revelation 12:11: *"And they overcame him by the blood of the Lamb and by the word of their testimony, and they did not love their lives to the death."*

My body is a temple for the Holy Spirit; redeemed, cleansed, and sanctified by the blood of Jesus. My members, the parts of my body, are instruments of righteousness, yielded to God for His service and for His glory. The devil has no place in me, no power over me, no unsettled claims against me. All has been settled by the blood of Jesus. I overcome Satan by the blood of the Lamb and by the word of my testimony, and I love not my life unto the death. My body is for the Lord, and the Lord is for my body.

Making these confessions regularly is a very practical way for us to apply the victory that Jesus won over Satan at the cross. They are included for your use not only in this chapter, but also at the end of chapter 13 and at the back of this book. (They bear repeating—*often.*)

CHAPTER 6

THE DOORWAY
TO HIDDEN WISDOM

The fifth reason the cross must be kept at the center of our lives is that it is the doorway to God's hidden wisdom. For this point, we again refer to 1 Corinthians 2:3, where Paul states that we do not rest our faith in the wisdom of this world. Following this, in verse 6, Paul begins to discuss a different sort of wisdom:

> *However, we speak wisdom among those who are mature, yet not the wisdom of this age, nor of the rulers of this age, who are coming to nothing. But we speak the wisdom of God in a mystery, the hidden wisdom which God ordained before the ages for our glory.*
>
> (1 Corinthians 2:6–7)

The *New English Bible* translation uses the phrase *"a secret, hidden wisdom of God."*

A SEARCH FOR WISDOM

In my early days as a philosopher, I was looking for a secret, hidden wisdom. In my church experience as a youth, I never found true wisdom in the Christianity I knew. Neither did I find it in my years of philosophical study. As my search continued, I looked for wisdom in yoga and in all sorts of improbable places without finding it.

Ultimately, I discovered that there is a door to wisdom that is shaped like a cross. If you go through the cross, you will find on the other side the secret, hidden wisdom of God. To me, it is exciting to have access to God's wisdom.

If this does not excite you, you may not fully understand what Paul is saying: *God has prepared a secret, hidden wisdom that is designed to bring us to glory.* His eternal plan to bring us to glory is contained in this secret, hidden wisdom. Again, if you go through the doorway of the cross, you will start to discover God's hidden wisdom.

Paul continues his discussion of this theme in 1 Corinthians 2:8–9:

> *Which none of the rulers of this age knew; for had they known, they would not have crucified the Lord of glory. But as it is written: "Eye has not seen, nor ear heard, nor have entered into the heart of man the things which God has prepared for those who love Him."*

The things of God cannot be discovered with the senses, with reason, or with the imagination. Paul tells us in verse 10,

> *But God has revealed them to us through His Spirit. For the Spirit searches all things, yes, the deep things of God.*

When we come through the door of the cross, the Holy Spirit begins to reveal to us what we could never find out by reasoning, by imagination, or by speculation. Such wisdom comes solely by revelation. The only entry point the Holy Spirit honors is the cross. If you come on any other basis, He is not interested. But when you make the cross central, He says, "That is a person I'm interested in."

I have made it my aim in life to engage in activities that attract the Holy Spirit. When the Holy Spirit is present, things go well. Over the years, I have discovered that to attract the Holy Spirit, we need to exalt Jesus and preach Christ crucified. When we engage in these activities, the Holy Spirit says, "I like those people. I feel at home with them. I'll participate in that meeting because it pleases me when Jesus is exalted."

LIFTED TO HEAVENLY PLACES

Here is Paul's own testimony of seeking heavenly revelation, as he gives it in Philippians 3. The testimony he provides in these verses refers to his life in Judaism and his inheritance as a religious Jew:

> But what things were gain to me, these I have counted loss for Christ. Yet indeed I also count all things loss for the excellence of the knowledge of Christ Jesus my Lord, for whom I have suffered the loss of all things, and count them as rubbish, that I may gain Christ and be found in Him, not having my own righteousness, which is from the law, but that which is through faith in Christ, the righteousness which is from God by faith [faith is the only basis

of righteousness]; *that I may know Him and the power of His resurrection, and the fellowship of His sufferings, being conformed to His death, if, by any means, I may attain to the resurrection from the dead.*

(Philippians 3:7–11)

Paul's supreme ambition was to know Jesus Christ. He did not write as somebody who did not know Christ—yet his desire was to know Him better. This longing to know Jesus was still Paul's yearning after many years of fruitful Christian service.

Paul states that he wants to know the power of Christ's resurrection. He also acknowledges that with that power comes *"the fellowship of His sufferings, being conformed to His death."* No cross—no crown. The cross is the way to the secret, hidden wisdom of God by which we share His glory.

What Paul says in Philippians 3 complements what he writes in Ephesians 2:4–6:

But God, who is rich in mercy, because of His great love with which He loved us, even when we were dead in trespasses, made us alive together with Christ (by grace you have been saved), and raised us up together, and made us sit together in the heavenly places in Christ Jesus.

The purpose of our redemption is to enable us to be in the heavenly places, seated with Christ. The Weymouth Bible translation says that God has *"enthroned us"* together with Christ. (See Ephesians 2:6.)

In a certain sense, when we come to the cross, it is like entering an elevator, or a lift. When you get inside an elevator, you press the button for whichever floor you want—and it takes you up to that floor. Once we are in Christ through His crucifixion and death, we are also made alive with Him and resurrected with Him. This is tremendous. But it is not the end—because the elevator stops at the throne. We are enthroned with Him! We do not get there by our own efforts. We get there because we are in the lift. However, the doorway to the lift is the cross. Only when we enter through the cross do we qualify for the throne.

LIGHT IN THE TABERNACLE

A similar picture of God's hidden wisdom is in the symbolism of the tabernacle of Moses. In the tabernacle, there were three distinct areas. One way each of these areas was distinguished was by the light available in each.

First, there was the outer court, where the light was natural: it was lit by the sun, the moon, and the stars. From the outer court, you would step through the first veil and enter what is called the Holy Place. Here you were not walking by natural light. The light in the Holy Place was supplied by a seven-branched lampstand fueled by olive oil. This lampstand represents the light of the inspired Word of God illuminated by the Holy Spirit.

However, the Holy Place is not your destination. Stepping through that first veil represents *resurrection* (being raised up with Christ). This requires a step of faith—because we do not walk by sight, but by faith in God's Word. (See 2 Corinthians 5:7.) But stepping through the second veil signifies *ascension*. Inside the second veil, in the Holy of Holies, was where the presence of God dwelt on the ark of the covenant. (See, for example, Isaiah 37:16.) This represents the heavenly throne.

It is from within the second veil that Jesus exercises His two supreme ministries as King and Priest. There is no candle or artificial light inside the Holy of Holies. It is totally dark. I wonder how many of us would make this our destination— just one little room, a cubicle with no light and just one item of furniture. Doesn't that sound exciting?

But this picture from the tabernacle is very vivid, because the further we go in the Christian life, the less there is to distract us. The only people who will go through the second veil are those who want just one thing: God Himself. Inside the second veil, if you meet the conditions, there comes a light that is not natural or artificial. It is the *shekinah glory*—the actual presence of God supernaturally illuminating everything. This is the secret, hidden wisdom of God.

GOING FURTHER WITH GOD

You do not have to go through the second veil; you can stop anywhere. Returning to the image of the elevator, you can press the button and get off at the mezzanine level or the second floor. However, there is something in me that wants to go as high as the lift will go. I have seen something in the lives of great men and women of God that, in a sense, I would characterize as a place of loneliness. It is a place where you are bereft of everything except God. But when you have God, you have everything.

This is the climax of Romans 8—where we are united with Christ, and nothing can separate us from His love. Paul says he cares nothing for the law or for his inheritance in Judaism. He cares nothing about the possessions he has lost. None of it matters, because all he wants is to be inside the second veil.

Like Paul, I want the revelation of Jesus Christ. I do not want mere theology or doctrine; I want a personal, intimate revelation of Jesus. That is the only reality that can fully satisfy the longing of our souls. Truly, the only pathway to it is through the cross.

As you read these words, a stirring may be taking place inside you. It may be a longing similar to what Paul expressed—to know Jesus in a more intimate way. Inside your heart, you may be yearning to step into the Holy of Holies—to go through the doorway of the cross and to move into the hidden wisdom of God.

You may not understand all the implications of what you are longing for. But you can still express it to the Lord with the following prayer:

> Lord Jesus, I want to go further with You. If the cross is the lift to take me there, I want to go as high as possible—to be enthroned with You in heavenly places. Thank You for the cross, the door to Your secret, hidden wisdom. Help me to find my way to that wisdom. Amen.

CHAPTER 7

THE ULTIMATE DEMONSTRATION OF GOD'S LOVE

W e will now consider the sixth and final reason why we must never allow the cross to be removed from the central position in our lives. Here it is: the cross is the ultimate demonstration of God's love for us and of our value to Him. In John 15:13–14, Jesus says to His disciples:

> Greater love has no one than this, than to lay down one's life for his friends. You are My friends if you do whatever I command you.

The supreme demonstration of one person's love for another is the willingness of that person to lay down his or her life for the other person. What Jesus is telling His disciples is that He is about to demonstrate the greatest love. He is going to lay down His life for His own dearest friends.

THE NATURE OF GOD'S LOVE

With this profound statement by Jesus as background, let's look at Romans 5:6–10. In this passage, Paul expounds upon the nature of God's love and the extent of His grace.

For when we were still without strength, in due time Christ died for the ungodly. For scarcely for a righteous man will one die; yet perhaps for a good man someone would even dare to die. But God demonstrates His own love toward us, in that while we were still sinners, Christ died for us. Much more then, having now been justified by His blood [notice the means of justification], *we shall be saved from wrath through Him. For if when we were enemies we were reconciled to God through the death of His Son, much more, having been reconciled, we shall be saved by His life.*

A quick analysis of this passage reveals four statements by Paul about the condition of human beings when Christ died for us. He says, first of all, we were *"without strength"* (verse 6). We could do absolutely nothing to help ourselves; we were totally dependent on God's mercy.

Second, Paul says Christ died for the *"ungodly"* (verse 6). We were ungodly; we had a nature and a way of life that offended God. We had a manner of thinking and conducting ourselves that was totally alien to His thoughts and ways.

Third, Paul writes that *"while we were still sinners, Christ died for us"* (verse 8). We were disobedient and rebellious—not in any sense seeking to please God.

Fourth and finally, he says that *"when we were enemies we were reconciled to God"* (verse 10). We naturally stood in full opposition to God and His ways.

Paul uses these four different phrases to describe our condition when Christ died for us. We were without strength, totally helpless. We were ungodly; everything about us was alien to God's nature. We were sinners, disobedient rebels. And we were enemies, actually in opposition to God. When we were in that condition, Christ died for us. That is the measure of God's love for us.

THE ASSURANCE OF GOD'S LOVE

It is very important that we fully comprehend the extent of God's love for us, because I regularly encounter Christians who are not really sure that God loves them. Perhaps you, also, have experienced some doubts about God's love for you. Those doubts will never be fully resolved until you have grasped the full measure of the condition you were in when Christ died for you.

God will not allow you to come to peace with Him on any grounds other than what Jesus did on the cross. You may be relying on the attitude of a friend or the help of a trusted minister for the assurance that you are truly loved by God. However, if I understand God's dealings, sooner or later, He will remove all other sources of assurance from your life. Why? Because He does not want you to base your understanding of His love on anything except the sacrifice of Jesus on the cross.

In times of darkness, you may find yourself wondering what is going on with you. In those times, God will illuminate only one point of reference in the darkness. What will that be? The cross, which is all you need to know in such circumstances. The trouble with many of us is that we know too much. God wants to bring us to the place where it is sufficient for us simply to know that Christ died for us.

THE MAGNITUDE OF GOD'S LOVE

In Romans 8, speaking of the magnitude of God's love, Paul writes:

> *Who shall separate us from the love of Christ? Shall tribulation, or distress, or persecution, or famine, or nakedness, or peril, or sword? As it is written: "For Your sake we are killed all day long; we are accounted as sheep for the slaughter."* (Romans 8:35–36)

We need to take note that when verse 36 talks about being sheep for the slaughter, it is God's people who are speaking. There are presently multitudes of Christians in different parts of the earth who are experiencing this type of persecution in a very literal way. In fact, there is no guarantee that one day you and I might not find ourselves in the same category. In spite of this fact, the promise remains true for them and for us: we cannot be separated from the love of Jesus Christ.

> *Yet in all these things we are more than conquerors through Him who loved us. For I am persuaded [convinced] that neither death nor life, nor angels nor principalities nor powers, nor things present nor things to come, nor height nor depth, nor any other created thing, shall be able to separate us from the love of God which is in Christ Jesus our Lord.* (Romans 8:37–39)

This is the climax of what I call the "Roman Pilgrimage," the spiritual journey Paul takes us on in the first eight chapters of Romans, culminating with the above passage. That climax is an inseparable, eternal union with Jesus Christ—being completely enveloped in His love forever.

OUR ASTOUNDING WORTH TO GOD

The cross is not only the demonstration of God's love for us. It is also the demonstration of our value and worth to Him. One of the most common problems psychologists deal with in their patients is a low sense of self-worth. I have found this to be a very common problem throughout the body of Christ, as well.

Actually, there is only one real basis for knowing your worth—and that is the cross. Most people would agree that the value of any item is based upon what people are willing to pay for it. For instance, suppose I want to sell my house for $200,000, and I put it on the market for that price. If nobody will pay more than $120,000 for it, then it is really worth no more than $120,000. My house is only worth what people would be willing to pay for it.

Let's extend this analogy to your value as a person. May I remind you that your value as a person is not what *you think* your value is? Rather, your value is what God is willing to pay for you. Amazingly, the price He paid to redeem you was the life of His Son, Jesus. There is nothing God could have given that would be of greater value. Therefore, our worth is greater than anything else in the universe. That fact should astound us!

An understanding of the blood of Jesus as our purchase price was always in the minds of the apostles. In Acts 20, Paul says, addressing the elders of the church in Ephesus:

> *Therefore take heed to yourselves and to all the flock, among which the Holy Spirit has made you overseers, to shepherd the church of God which He purchased with His own blood.*   (Acts 20:28)

Please note: it was the blood of God that purchased the church—that is, the blood of God through Jesus. In similar fashion, Peter writes:

> *Knowing that you were not redeemed with corruptible things, like silver or gold, from your aimless conduct received by tradition from your fathers, but with the precious blood of Christ, as of a lamb without blemish and without spot.*   (1 Peter 1:18–19)

"*Without blemish*" means without original sin, and "*without spot*" means without personal sin. As Peter attests, our entire redemption is accomplished through one means: the blood of Jesus. Leviticus 17:11 says that the life, or soul, of the flesh is in the blood—which God told the Israelites He had given to them upon the altar to make atonement for their souls.

Prophetically, Isaiah 53:12 tells us Jesus poured out His life, or His soul, "*unto death.*" When Jesus poured out His blood on the cross, He gave His life—His soul—as the redemption price for all of humanity.

The price was more than was needed, because one perfect, divine life was worth more than all the lives of all humanity for all ages of history. That life was paid in full to buy us back out of the hand of the devil. We are redeemed, the Bible says, by the blood of Jesus. (See, for example, Ephesians 1:7; 1 Peter 1:18–19.) By that token, the cross where Jesus poured out His blood is the ultimate demonstration of God's love for us and of our value to Him.

THE PEARL IN GOD'S HAND

Jesus' parable of the merchant buying pearls is a beautiful picture of the love that God has for us. There are many ways to interpret this parable, and you may have your own favorite. But please bear with me as I share my thoughts on it. The interpretation I am about to give is very real and personal to me.

> *The kingdom of heaven is like a merchant seeking beautiful pearls, who, when he had found one pearl of great price, went and sold all that he had and bought it.*
> (Matthew 13:45–46)

To me, this parable pictures Jesus as the merchant. He knew the value of pearls—He was a professional. He saw one pearl so valuable that He sold all He had to possess it.

From a purely human, modern perspective, I like to imagine the merchant coming home to his wife and explaining his purchase.

The merchant's wife says, "Why did you walk home from the office?"

He replies, "Well, I sold the car."

"Sold the car! Whatever for?"

"Not only that, but I've also sold the house."

"You sold our house! We'll have to move to the farm."

"No, I've sold the farm, too. I've sold everything we own."

"You sold everything? Are you crazy? Why in the world would you do such a thing?"

"Because I found something so valuable it was worth everything."

"What was it?"

He opens his palm and says, "This pearl. It's worth everything we ever owned."

What is that pearl? The pearl of great value is *you*. One human soul. If nobody else had ever been saved in all of history, Jesus would have died just for you.

If you have any doubts about your worth to God, think of yourself as that pearl in the hand of the Lord. Right now, I want you to hear Him saying to you, "I gave everything I had to purchase you. That's how much you mean to Me. Don't ever say again that you're not worth much. Because, in My sight, you're worth everything. Yes, I gave everything I ever had. You are so beautiful, so perfect—I know how valuable you are. Everything I sold just didn't add up to what you mean to Me. You are the pearl in My hand."

If you can believe what I have just shared, it will change your life. Do not let the world dictate to you what you are worth—because you are worth exactly what God paid for you.

Here, again, is the list of all six reasons why the cross must be kept central in the life of the church and in our lives personally:

1. The cross is the one perfect, all-sufficient sacrifice, removing the guilt of all humanity.

2. Through the cross, supernatural grace is released.

3. Through the cross, there is a release of God's supernatural signs and miracles.

4. The cross is the sole basis of the total defeat of Satan.

5. The cross is the door to God's secret, hidden wisdom.

6. The cross is the ultimate demonstration of God's love for us and our value to Him.

As a way of closing this chapter and part 1 of this book, let's take just a moment to thank the Lord. Especially when we consider the magnitude of God's love for us, we have great cause to give thanks.

Thank You, Lord, for the cross. Thank You for everything that has been released in my life through all that Jesus accomplished on the cross. I receive it all—especially the truth covered in this chapter. On the cross, You demonstrated Your love for me and for all people everywhere. Through the cross, You let me know my value in Your sight. I stand amazed—and I bow in gratitude to You for Your great love for me. Amen.

PART TWO

THE CROSS IN MY LIFE

CHAPTER 8

SATAN'S STRATEGY: OBSCURING THE CROSS

In the second part of this book, we will focus on how the work of the cross is applied in a practical way in our lives. As the foundation for our discussion, let us summarize the work of the cross by saying that *the cross is the basis of God's total provision for every believer.* Everything has been provided for us through the cross. All we will ever need, in time and eternity, in every department of our lives—spiritual, mental, emotional, physical, financial, temporal, or eternal—comes to us through the cross. There is no other basis. Either we receive on the basis of the cross, or we simply do not receive.

In Romans 8:32, Paul says, *"He who did not spare His own Son, but delivered Him up for us all, how shall He not with Him also freely give us all things?"* Try to absorb these words. God, through Jesus, will freely give us all things. But without Jesus—nothing. On the basis of the cross, we can receive everything. But without that basis, we are not entitled to anything.

We must also remember that the cross is the basis of Christ's total defeat of Satan. Through His substitutionary sacrifice and death, His victorious resurrection, and His triumphant ascension, Jesus has administered to Satan and his kingdom a total, eternal, and irrevocable defeat. There is nothing Satan can ever do to change that fact. And as a result of the cross, we can have victory over the enemy. If we do battle with Satan on any basis other than the cross, we will be defeated. However, on the foundation of what Jesus accomplished through the cross, we can be totally victorious.

LOSING SIGHT OF JESUS' VICTORY

Because of the two important facts we have just cited concerning the cross—that it is the basis of God's total provision and the basis of Satan's total defeat—the enemy has enacted a strategy against the church. In order for us to apply the victory of Jesus effectively in our lives in a daily, practical way, it is necessary for us to be keenly aware of this strategy and how to overcome it.

We have noted that when Jesus was crucified, Satan at first imagined that he had gained a tremendous victory. However, to his chagrin, he soon discovered that just the opposite had occurred. Satan suddenly realized that through Jesus' death at Calvary, all his claims had been cancelled, and all his power had been taken from him. He could not change what had been accomplished by the cross. That was eternal, settled forever by God Almighty.

If you were in Satan's position, having discovered that through the sacrifice of Jesus on the cross everything you had been seeking to achieve had been thwarted, what would you do? In his own twisted way, Satan is very astute. In the face of this reality, he knew that his only option would be to obscure the work and power of the cross, doing his utmost to keep people from realizing what Jesus accomplished for them at Calvary. (We began to expose this strategy when we discussed Satan as the accuser of the brethren, attempting to make us feel guilty and condemned rather than forgiven and free.)

When we as Christians lose sight of the victory Jesus won for us at Calvary, we can no longer seek and experience the benefits provided by the cross. Further, when the power of the cross is obscured, we are no longer capable of administering Christ's defeat to Satan.

This is precisely the strategy the devil has sought to implement for nearly two thousand years. In fact, I believe most of the major problems of the church occur when Satan is able to obscure what Jesus has accomplished for us by His death on the cross.

"WHO HAS BEWITCHED YOU?"

Satan's strategy is expressed very clearly by Paul in his letter to the Galatians. We read these sobering words in Galatians 3:1:

> O foolish Galatians! Who has bewitched you that you should not obey the truth, before whose eyes Jesus Christ was clearly portrayed among you as crucified?

I have meditated on this verse for many years. When I first read it, like so many verses in the Bible, I just read it and took note of it, but I did not think much about it. Gradually, however, this verse impacted me more and more. I have come to see these words as a key to understanding the problems of Christians in the church today.

Paul makes an amazing statement to these Galatian Christians who have been saved and baptized in the Spirit, and who have witnessed miracles. He writes, *"Who has bewitched you?"*

Witchcraft is the primary word describing the release into the earth of spiritual forces from Satan's kingdom. Paul is saying to the Galatians that they have come under the influence of these powers.

Please understand that the Galatians were what we would call "Spirit-filled" Christians. When I hear the word *Spirit-filled*, and I see the lives of some people, I think, "Yes, they are filled, but just a thimbleful." You can fill a thimble, you can fill a cup, or you can fill a bathtub. All of them are filled—but they do not contain the same amount. There are many Spirit-filled Christians who do not realize Satan has implemented his strategy against them. They are totally unaware that they have been "bewitched."

In 1963, I found myself in a situation where this kind of deception was vividly portrayed to me. I had just immigrated to the United States with my first wife, Lydia, and our five-year-old adopted black African daughter. The assignment bringing us to America was for Lydia and me to pastor a Pentecostal church in Seattle, Washington.

I will not go into great detail covering the problems of that church, but I will provide enough background to show what can happen to Spirit-filled believers. Prior to our arrival at this church, the wife of the previous pastor had fallen in love with one of the members of the church board. As a result, the pastor's wife had divorced the pastor, and the board member had divorced his wife. The pastor's wife and the board member had then married and continued to pastor the church together for a time.

All this was publicly known; there was no secret about it. By the time we arrived in Seattle, the woman had moved out—but the congregation was still under her domination. When I would talk with the congregants about the situation, they would say to me, "There's something about that woman. When she looks at me, my blood runs cold and I just don't know what to say."

This woman had actually gained total control over that congregation. Lydia and I had never been in a situation like that, and I began to seek God because we had no idea what to do about it. It was at that time that the Lord led me to this verse: *"Foolish Galatians! Who has bewitched you...?"*

I said, "That's it. They are bewitched!"

At first, I could not believe Christians could be bewitched. However, when Lydia and I grasped the truth and took a stand, agreeing together in prayer, we broke that power. As a result, the congregation was released, and the church situation was restored to spiritual health.

RESULTS OF THE OBSCURED CROSS

How did Paul know the Galatians were bewitched? The second part of Galatians 3:1 tells us: *they had lost the vision of Jesus Christ crucified.* A satanic power had moved into that once vigorous, spiritual church and robbed them of their understanding of the cross. Witchcraft had obscured the reality of the cross and all that Jesus had obtained for them through it.

As a result of losing their vision of the crucified Christ, the Galatians fell into carnality and legalism. Generally, wherever you find legalism, it is the product of carnality. Even though keeping rules and laws sounds extremely spiritual, it is still an expression of the flesh. It is not a characteristic linked with spirituality.

Paul continues:

This only I want to learn from you: Did you receive the Spirit by the works of the law, or by the hearing of faith? Are you so foolish? Having begun in the Spirit, are you now being made perfect by the flesh? Have you suffered so many things in vain—if indeed it was in vain? Therefore He who supplies the Spirit to you and works miracles among you, does He do it by the works of the law, or by the hearing of faith? (Galatians 3:2–5)

Please notice these facts: the Galatians were saved and baptized in the Spirit, and God was working miracles among them. Yet they were bewitched. In this passage, Paul talks about the two results we have attributed to losing sight of the cross. What are they again? The works of the law and the works of the flesh—in other words, legalism and carnality.

I would define legalism as *the attempt to achieve righteousness with God by observing any set of rules whatsoever.* It makes no difference if it is the law of Moses, some denominational regulation, or a personal moral code. Anyone who is seeking to achieve righteousness with God by observing a law or a set of rules is in legalism.

An alternative definition of legalism is *to add anything to the requirements God has laid down for achieving righteousness with Him.* God declares that His righteousness is given to us if we believe that He delivered Jesus to death for our offenses and raised Him again for our justification. (See Romans 4:24–25.)

No pastor, church, organization, or Bible teacher has the authority to add any requirement to achieving righteousness with God apart from faith. By my understanding, any requirement in addition to believing in the One who delivered Jesus for our sins and raised Him for our justification is legalism.

The Galatians had been tricked by Satan because he had succeeded in obscuring the reality of what took place on the cross. As a result, these believers had gone back into fleshly attempts to please God by keeping rules, which in their case were the Jewish laws.

The Threat of a Curse

The ramifications of this deception in the Galatian church are shocking. As Galatians 3:10 points out,

*For as many as are of the works of the law are under the
curse; for it is written, "Cursed is everyone who does not
continue in all things which are written in the book of the
law, to do them."*   (Galatians 3:10)

The reality that most people do not understand is that
to be justified by the law of Moses, one must keep the *whole*
law *all* the time. If you put yourself under the law and fail to
observe every aspect of it, you bring a curse upon yourself.
Why? Because the law itself says that everyone who does not
keep *all* the law *all* the time is cursed.

In Galatia, the results of the cross being obscured by
Satan's activities were legalism, carnality, and a curse. This is a
very solemn thought.

For further insight into what was taking place with the
Galatians, we can turn to Jeremiah 17:5:

*Thus says the LORD: "Cursed is the man who trusts in
man and makes flesh his strength, whose heart departs
from the LORD."*

The curse is pronounced on anyone *"whose heart departs
from the LORD."* If, like the Galatians, a group of people begins
in the supernatural blessing and power of God, having the
Holy Spirit move and work through their lives, producing the
results that He alone can produce, and then those people go
back to their own efforts, with their own plans, organization,
and programs, what are they saying to God? "God, it was nice
to have the Holy Spirit with us, but we think we'll do better

without Him." Those people are snubbing the Spirit of God. That is why He pronounces a curse!

The next verse is a vivid portrayal of somebody under a curse:

> *For he shall be like a shrub in the desert, and shall not see when good comes, but shall inhabit the parched places in the wilderness, in a salt land which is not inhabited.*
>
> (Jeremiah 17:6)

For the man in this verse, blessings are all around him, but they never reach him. The rain falls around him, and the surrounding land is fruitful. But he lives in a dry, barren, cursed land.

Ever since God gave me an understanding of how a curse operates and how people can be delivered from it, I have dealt with hundreds of people who were under a curse. In most of these cases, I have seen them delivered and restored to a place of blessing.

A Widespread Problem

I challenge you to consider the problem of the Galatians as I have described it. Could it be that you have the same problem in your life? Could it be the problem that is afflicting your church? Could it perhaps be the primary problem of the professing church today?

Almost every major denomination in the church began with a supernatural visitation of God. Otherwise, they never would have impacted history. No matter which denomination you consider, it began because God visited them sovereignly with supernatural power. Tragically, however, very few of these denominations are currently relying on the same sovereign, supernatural power that gave them birth. Like the Galatians, they began in the Spirit but are seeking to be perfected in the flesh. (See Galatians 3:3.)

I underscore this point because the issue we are dealing with here is something that is real, current, and extremely important. This is not some obscure problem operating in a remote little group somewhere that has gone astray. We are uncovering Satan's destructive strategy against the church of Jesus Christ. What is Satan's main weapon again? *To obscure the reality of the cross.*

Evidence of Soulishness

Generally, as I understand it, the result of losing our vision of what Jesus accomplished for us on the cross is the substitution of the soulish for the spiritual. Man consists of spirit, soul, and body, and the soul has its legitimate functions. However, it cannot take the place of the spirit. When people move away from the supernatural and begin to rely on their own ability and efforts, they move out of the spiritual and into the soulish.

The following list contains seven different ways that soulishness manifests itself in the church. These are examples of how religious substitutes can take the place of spiritual reality.

1. Theology takes the place of revelation. Theology uses man's reason to develop principles and doctrines. But it is not the same as direct revelation from God.

2. Education takes the place of character building. Jesus did not simply talk with people. He challenged them to follow Him. In other words, He did not just give intellectual knowledge. He imparted a lifestyle. It is dangerous to train people intellectually but neglect to train them in developing their character as well.

3. The Scripture says, *"The carnal mind is enmity against God"* (Romans 8:7). When we merely educate the carnal mind, we are educating an enemy of God. Many seminaries today are producing educated enemies of God. By saying this, I am not trying to be dramatic. I just believe it is a fact. Some of the main enemies of the true gospel of the kingdom are the products of seminaries.

4. Psychology is substituted for supernatural discernment.

5. Programs are substituted for the supernatural leading of the Holy Spirit, as well as the supernatural gifts and ministries of the Spirit.

6. Eloquence is substituted for supernatural power with signs and miracles.

7. Reasoning is substituted for the walk of faith.

8. Laws take the place of love as the standard for conduct.

Legalism

The last point brings our focus back to the topic of legalism. If you happen to know any Christians whom you would categorize as legalistic, would you say they are very loving? In the Christian life, laws and love tend to compete with one another. The people who are busy keeping and enforcing laws are often remarkably unloving. The standard biblical example of this reality is the Pharisees.

In reading the New Testament, have you noticed how the Pharisees objected to many of the miracles that Jesus performed? Blind eyes were opened and lame people walked. Yet the Pharisees never once expressed any appreciation for the mercy of God. On the contrary, they objected to Jesus breaking their rules of the Sabbath. You would think even a Pharisee with a heart of stone would be glad when somebody who was born blind had his eyes opened. Yet in this case and many others, legalism won out over love.

The apostle Paul was much more disturbed by legalism than by open sin, because it is a much subtler and more dangerous problem. When Paul became aware of the problem in Galatia, he did not write a theological treatise. He sat down immediately and dashed off a letter in his own handwriting (see Galatians 6:11) because he was so deeply concerned about them.

In Paul's letters to other churches, he almost invariably begins by thanking God for the churches to whom he is writing. Even in his letter to the church at Corinth—where there was incest, adultery, and drunkenness at the Lord's

Table—he still begins by thanking God for the grace given to the Corinthians. However, when he writes to the Galatians, he is so upset that he does not thank God for them. Instead, he bluntly says, "I marvel that you have so soon moved away from the grace of God." (See Galatians 1:6.)

No doubt, what I have presented in this chapter about Satan's strategy and its outworkings can have a disturbing effect upon us. In our next chapter, however, we will move from the matter of Satan's attempts to obscure the power of the cross to God's solution—a powerful revelation of the cross of Jesus Christ.

CHAPTER 9

FREEDOM FROM
THE PRESENT EVIL AGE

THE CROSS IN US

Paul's letter to the Galatians not only reveals the dangers of losing sight of the cross, but it also reveals God's solution for it. I have entitled part 2 of this book "The Cross in My Life" because the victory Jesus accomplished at Calvary needs to be very personal to you as you read this. It is one thing to get excited about what God has done for us through the cross. However, it can be quite a different matter for each of us to *embrace what the cross is intended to do in us.*

In many churches, very little is mentioned about what the cross is intended to do in us. In my opinion, the majority of the church's problems are due to the neglect of the work of Calvary as it applies to us personally. In the long run, we will not enjoy the benefits of what the cross has done *for* us unless we accept what the cross is intended to do *in* us. The cross *in us* is the safeguard of all the blessings and provisions of the cross *for us.*

In Galatians, Paul presents five very practical deliverances that are provided for us through the power of the cross working in us. Through that power, we are delivered from:

1. this present evil age;

2. the law as a means of righteousness;

3. the tyranny of self;

4. the flesh;

5. and, finally, the world.

In this chapter and the ones to follow, we will consider each of these deliverances in detail.

THE END OF THIS AGE

The first deliverance that we will discuss is stated in Galatians 1:3–4:

> Grace to you and peace from God the Father and our Lord Jesus Christ, who gave Himself for our sins, that He might deliver us from this present evil age, according to the will of our God and Father.

Through the cross, God has provided deliverance for us from this present evil age. I would suggest that a vast majority of believers have never even thought about the need for this deliverance. One of the reasons I say this is because I went a long while as a Christian and as a preacher without thinking about it myself!

The King James translation of the above uses the phrase "this present evil **world**." The Greek word rendered "world" is *aion*, from which we get the English word *eon*. Basically, it means an age as a period of time. Most modern versions translate the phrase as "this present evil *age*," as does the *New King James*, the version I am primarily using in this book.

So the Scripture says we are living in a certain time, which Paul calls *"this present evil age."* There were other ages before this one, and there will be ages after this. Of course, this means that the present age is going to come to an end. When I realize the present age is going to end, I thank God—I would not want this age to continue the way it is forever.

Jesus spoke very clearly about the end of the age in His parables in Matthew 13. We will not examine these parables in detail; I will simply quote three verses from them that use the phrase "the end of the (or this) age." The first two are from Jesus' explanation of the parable of the wheat and the tares:

> *The enemy who sowed them is the devil, the harvest is the*
> **end of the age**....   (Matthew 13:39)

> *Therefore as the tares are gathered and burned in the fire,*
> *so it will be at the* **end of this age**.   (Matthew 13:40)

The third is from Jesus' explanation of the parable of the dragnet:

> *So it will be at the* **end of the age**.   (Matthew 13:49)

Thus, it is important for us to keep in mind that this present age in which we live is going to end. It is not permanent.

THE GOD OF THIS AGE

The reason why Paul refers to this age as "evil" is explained in 2 Corinthians 4:3–4:

> But even if our gospel is veiled, it is veiled to those who are perishing, whose minds **the god of this age** has blinded, who do not believe, lest the light of the gospel of the glory of Christ, who is the image of God, should shine on them.

It is an evil age because it is ruled by the deceitful and malevolent "god of this age." The god of this age who has blinded the minds of so many people is Satan. Satan does not want this age to end, because as long as this age continues, he is a "god." When this age comes to an end, he will cease to be a god. Therefore, he is doing everything in his power to delay the close of the age.

As Christians, what should be our response to this strategy of the enemy? In direct opposition to Satan, the church should be doing everything in its power to precipitate the close of the age. As we have already discussed, however, if Satan can blind the minds of most Christians concerning his plan, we will not do what God expects the church to do to bring about the close of the age.

Jesus told His disciples, "This gospel of the kingdom will be preached in all the world as a witness to all the nations, and then the end will come" (Matthew 24:14). The age will not come to an end until the gospel of the kingdom of God has been proclaimed to every people group on the earth. This is one way that the church can hasten the closing of this present evil age.

We should be continually striving toward this end, recognizing that Satan is totally committed to preventing the declaration of the kingdom and the message of Christ crucified from being proclaimed.

THE AGE TO COME

In Hebrews 6:4–6, the writer of Hebrews speaks about people who have received a series of experiences. Beginning in verse 4, he writes:

> ...*those who were once enlightened, and have tasted the heavenly gift, and have become partakers of the Holy Spirit, and have tasted the good word of God and the powers of the age to come.*

Notice that when we become partakers of the Holy Spirit, we taste the powers of the next age. By our experience in the Holy Spirit, we are lifted out of the present age. We begin to experience, in a little way, what it will be like to be in the next age.

Let me explain this concept a little further. Paul says in 1 Corinthians 15:44 that the body we have in this age is a "soulish" body. Many of our English translations use the term *"natural"* body, with most of the other versions using the word *"physical"* body. But the Greek word is *psuchikos*, which would be best translated as "soulish."

In other words, we presently have a body that operates as our soul directs it. Therefore, if my spirit wants my body to do something, my spirit must work through my soul. When

David wanted to praise the Lord with his mouth, his spirit spoke to his soul and said, *"Bless the LORD, O my soul"* (Psalm 103:2). David's spirit could not start blessing the Lord without the cooperation of the soul. Why? Because he had a soulish body. (This is a slightly different use of the word *soulish* than we discussed in the last chapter, where "soulish" referred to the soul operating independent of the spirit's influence; again, the soul should never take precedence over the spirit but instead must allow the spirit to direct it.)

Paul says that in the next age we will have a spiritual body. According to my understanding, having a spiritual body will mean that our spirit directly controls our body. We will not need to operate through our soul. For example, if I decide to travel to some other city, I will simply do so. I will not have to argue with my soul about the rights and wrongs of the journey.

The point here is that when you are baptized in the Holy Spirit, you taste the powers of the age to come. When you speak in other tongues as the Spirit gives you utterance, your spirit is directly controlling your tongue. Your tongue does not need to go through the bottleneck of your mind. This is one reason why speaking in tongues is such a significant experience. For most of us, it is one of the main ways in which we can enter into what it will be like to live in the next age.

Although I do not need to use my mind when I speak in tongues (see 1 Corinthians 14:14), my soul must consent to it. If my soul says, "No, I don't want to speak in tongues; I don't understand what I'm saying," then my spirit will not be able to speak. But if my soul has surrendered to my spirit, then when I want to speak in tongues, I can. When I speak in tongues, my mind does not know what I am saying. But I know it is good, because the Holy Spirit gave it. When you speak in the Spirit, your tongue does what it was always supposed to do: it glorifies the Lord. You will never say one wrong word as long as the Holy Spirit is controlling your tongue.

Presently, we can only taste of the coming age. However, let us remember that there is going to be a different way of living in the next age. Our spirit is going to be in direct control of our body, and we will not be limited by our souls and the dictates of our minds.

THE CARES OF THIS AGE

Returning to the parables of Matthew 13, we find another problem connected with this present age. In Matthew 13:22, Jesus is interpreting the parable of the sower. In doing so, He speaks about the seed that fell on soil that was infested with thorns:

> *Now he who received seed among the thorns is he who hears the word, and the cares of this world and the deceitfulness of riches choke the word, and he becomes unfruitful.*

The above Scripture uses the phrase *"of this world"*—but, again, the Greek word translated *"world"* is *aion*, which is more accurately rendered "age." Jesus said that this age has *"cares."* When we are too preoccupied with the cares of the present age, that preoccupation makes the Word of God unfruitful in us. Why? Because a preoccupation with the affairs of this world chokes out the Word of God.

In Romans 12:2, Paul writes, *"And do not be conformed to this world* [Greek, *aion,* "age"], *but be transformed by the renewing of your mind."* We are not to think the way the people of this age think. We must learn to think differently. The people of this age are essentially *self-centered.* I believe that description is universally true—applying to almost everyone.

The attitude of this age is, "What will I get out of this?" However, those whose minds have been renewed think instead about what God wants. Their own lives are no longer the center. Their lives have become God-centered.

In the final analysis, as faithful servants of Christ, we cannot love this present age. Paul's second letter to Timothy was written near the end of the apostle's life. At that time, Paul was in prison, awaiting trial and probable execution. He had just a few faithful coworkers who had stuck with him, and one whom he had been counting on was named Demas. But Paul makes this sad and tragic statement concerning him: *"For Demas has forsaken me, having loved this present world* [*aion,* "age"]" (2 Timothy 4:10).

If you love this present age, you cannot be faithful to God. Let me ask you some questions: Are you in any way in love with this present age? Have you put all your eggs in the basket of this age? It is important to consider this question, because one day the whole basket is going to drop, and all the eggs will be smashed. Are you living as if this present age were going to go on forever?

These are very searching questions, but ones that we must face honestly before God. The cross of Jesus Christ empowers us to be free from the attraction of this present evil age. Are we walking in that freedom?

CHAPTER 10

FREEDOM FROM THE LAW

Paul writes, *"For I through the law died to the law that I might live to God"* (Galatians 2:19). The second deliverance that the cross provides is *freedom from the law*. I have spent many hours trying to persuade Christians of the reality of this deliverance, though I question how successful I have been. It is my observation that this is probably the hardest point for Christians to understand.

DYING TO THE LAW

"For I through the law died to the law." Why does Paul describe freedom from the law in this way? Because the law inflicted the death penalty on us. It was the law that caused us to be put to death. And, when we were put to death, our death became the end of the law for us.

The last punishment the law can inflict upon someone is to put them to death. Once that has happened, the individual is clear of the law. It does not matter if they committed one murder or sixty murders. If they have been executed, the law can do nothing more to them.

As we've previously discussed, death is the only way out from being under the law. However, through the marvelous mercy and grace of God, our "execution" took place twenty centuries ago. When Jesus died, we died in Him. (See Galatians 2:20.) Jesus paid the final penalty of the law on our behalf, so that we might be clear from the demands of the law.

Colossians 2:14 tells us that the law was nailed to the cross. Law cannot go beyond the cross. It can pursue you, it can hound you, it can accuse you, and it can condemn you. Yet it can follow you only as far as the cross. Once you get beyond the cross, you are free from the law. There is no more condemnation, because you have died to the law. We will discuss this theme in more detail later in this chapter.

THE LAW IS NOT OF FAITH

Paul says that through the law, he died to the law, that he might live to God. If you analyze what Paul has said, the meaning is clear: *If you are living to the law, you are not living to God; and if you're living to God, you are not living to the law.* You cannot have it both ways; you cannot combine the two. This is one of the clearest and most repeated statements of the New Testament. Even so, many Christians are completely unfamiliar with this principle.

Immediately after I was saved, I began to see that the relationship between the law and grace is the single most decisive issue in the New Testament. Sorting out this issue is not altogether simple for many people. I think the difficulty comes from the fact that we are not used to thinking God's way. It's not that this matter is overly complicated, but it does require a total adjustment of our thinking.

At the end of the Scripture we looked at earlier concerning the Galatians being under a curse because they had been bewitched, Paul states:

> But that no one is justified by the law in the sight of God is evident, for "the just shall live by faith." Yet the law is not of faith, but "the man who does them shall live by them."
> (Galatians 3:11–12)

In this passage, as in most similar verses in the New Testament that refer to "*the law*," the original Greek simply says "law." In many places, it makes a difference—and this passage is one of them. Therefore, it should read: "But that no one is justified by law in the sight of God is evident."

Paul's primary argument has been that we will not be justified by keeping the law of Moses. But he does not stop there. He says you cannot achieve righteousness with God by keeping *any law*. It is ruled out. It is impossible. Do not waste your time trying.

Paul says that if you can keep the whole law all the time, then you are righteous. However, as discussed earlier, with the exception of Jesus, nobody has ever kept the law perfectly. If you manage to keep a little of the law some of the time, it does you no good whatsoever in achieving righteousness. You must keep the *whole* law *all* of the time.

The apostle James confirms this principle when he writes, *"For whoever shall keep the whole law, and yet stumble in one point, he is guilty of all"* (James 2:10).

Therefore, you have two alternatives: either you are justified by law or you are justified by faith. It's either law or grace. But you cannot mix them.

Paul further illustrates this truth with a little parable from the family of Abraham. He gives the example of Ishmael, who was the child of the slave woman, Hagar. Ishmael is a type of what is produced by the law, because Hagar corresponds to Mount Sinai where the law was given. Sarah, however, is a type of the Spirit, having supernaturally conceived and brought forth Isaac, who is the child of grace. (See Galatians 4:21–31.)

Paul points out that when Isaac came, Ishmael had to go. They could not coexist in the same family. Quoting Genesis 21:10, he writes, *"Cast out the bondwoman and her son"* (Galatians 4:30). Sarah made this request of Abraham, and God told Abraham to do it.

Please notice a further implication from this verse: you must not only get rid of Ishmael, but you must also get rid of Hagar. You must choose whom you are going to have in your house. Are you going to keep Ishmael, or are you going to make room for Isaac, the child of supernatural grace?

Ishmael was the best that Abraham could do by his own wisdom and strength—but the result was not good enough. Likewise, the best we can do by our wisdom and strength is never good enough to fulfill God's purposes. We can keep on trying, sweating, working, and even praying. But in the end, it will never be good enough.

If you want grace, you must say no to law. Most of us would like to hold on to both—a little bit of grace and a little bit of law. However, God says it will not work. He will not accept a mixture. If you cannot trust grace wholly, then you are not trusting grace at all. If you must supplement grace with law, you are not really experiencing grace.

EXECUTION REQUIRED

In Romans 6, Paul explains how this deliverance from the law comes to us:

> *Knowing this, that our old man was crucified with Him, that the body of sin might be done away with, that we should no longer be slaves of sin. For he who has died has been freed from sin.*   (Romans 6:6–7)

Our *"old man"* was crucified when Jesus died on the cross. That is a historical fact that we cannot change. However, knowing it and believing it will change *us*. We are dealing with facts. Unlike almost any other world religion, the gospel of the kingdom is based on historical facts.

I do not know of any other world religion that is so completely based on events that took place in history. Other religions are systems, theories, or revelations not tied to any particular period of history. But the gospel is based on the historical facts of the life, death, burial, and resurrection of

Jesus Christ. (See, for example, 1 Corinthians 15:3–7.) This is important, because our death with Christ is based on a historical event—the death of Jesus.

Paul says that until this old nature—the Adamic nature, the rebel whom Paul calls the *"old man"*—has been put to death, we will be slaves of sin.

This old man—the flesh—is the nature we inherited because we are descendants of Adam. Adam never begot any children before he was in rebellion. However, all descendants of Adam from then on have in themselves the nature of a rebel. There is only one solution to this dilemma, only one way to deal with the old man, because at heart he is a rebel. What is it? God's solution is *execution*.

God does not try to improve the old man. He does not send him to church. He does not try to teach him the Golden Rule. He executes him! The good news is that by the mercy of God, this execution took place when Jesus died on the cross.

JUSTIFICATION FROM SIN

Paul completes his thought when he writes, *"For he who has died has been freed from sin."* This translation of Romans 6:7 is followed in almost every version of the Bible. But if we translate it literally from the Greek text, it reads, "…has been justified from sin." We are freed because once we have paid the last penalty, we are justified.

Once we are dead, the law has nothing more to say to us. It can do nothing more against us. Thus, death is the only way out from the dominion of the law. It is also the only way out from the dominion of sin.

Paul expands upon this truth in Romans 6:14: *"For sin shall not have dominion over you, for you are not under law but under grace."* Are you under law or under grace? You cannot be under both. If you are under law, you are *not* under grace. If you are under grace, you are *not* under law. Paul very clearly implies in verse 14 that if you are under law, sin *will* have dominion over you. This realization astonishes people, but that is the way it works.

ABSOLUTE DELIVERANCE

In Romans 7:5, Paul explains why this is so:

For when we were in the flesh, the sinful passions which were aroused by the law were at work in our members to bear fruit to death.

Notice the phrase *"the sinful passions which were aroused by the law were at work in our members."* Paul speaks personally about this in Romans 7:7–8, where he says, in effect, "I didn't know what covetousness was until I encountered the commandment 'Thou shalt not covet.' But when the commandment came, covetousness rose up in me."

Everyone has had this experience. As soon as we are told not to do something, that is when the desire to do it begins to gain dominion over us. The sin is actually stirred up by the law as long as we are relying on our own efforts.

Yet Paul says in Romans 7:6:

> *But now we have been delivered from the law, having died*
> *to what we were held by, so that we should serve in the*
> *newness of the Spirit and not in the oldness of the letter.*
> (Romans 7:6)

Let's be very clear on this point. Paul is not talking here about civil law. Being delivered from the law does not mean we can break the laws of the government. In fact, Paul tells Christians they should be law-abiding citizens. Rather, in this verse, Paul is referring to law as a means of achieving righteousness with God. That is the entire theme of this chapter—and here is the wonderful truth we have discovered: the cross provides us with absolute deliverance from the law.

DEATH RELEASES US

In the opening verses of Romans 7, Paul explains our freedom from the law by using the example of a married woman. If she marries another man while her husband remains alive, she is an adulteress. However, if her husband dies, she is free to marry another man.

Paul's application for you and me is that the husband to whom we were first espoused was the fleshly nature. Coming under the law is like a marriage ceremony in which we are married to our fleshly nature.

The covenant of the law requires us to rely on our own ability to obey it, because the law works through the flesh. So again, if we are under the law, we are married to the flesh. As long as the fleshly nature is alive, we are bound to the law and cannot be married to another. But at the cross, our fleshly nature was put to death. Therefore, we are now free to be married to another—to the resurrected Christ.

When we were married to the flesh, we brought forth the product of the flesh. Now that we are married to the resurrected Christ, what we bring forth is the product of the Spirit.

In 2 Corinthians 3:3 (NIV), Paul makes this statement:

You show that you are a letter from Christ, the result of our ministry, written not with ink but with the Spirit of the living God, not on tablets of stone but on tablets of human hearts.

Paul could say, "If you want to know my theology, go to Corinth. You'll find it written there in the lives of the people to whom I've ministered. In Corinth you will meet people who once were fornicators, adulterers, pimps, homosexuals, drunkards, and extortionists, but now are living godly lives. That's my theology. They're my letter."

WRITTEN ON OUR HEARTS

In 2 Corinthians 3:3, Paul touches the heart of the difference between law and grace. The law consists of tablets of stone outside of us that say, "Do this," and "Don't do that." Our reply to these instructions is, "All right. I'll do this, and I won't do that." However, we invariably fail, because there is a rebel inside us who will not submit to the law of God.

Grace, on the other hand, is totally different. Grace does not hold something up outside of us that tells us what to do. Instead, grace writes the laws of God on our hearts by the power of the Holy Spirit working in us. When something is in our hearts, that is the way we will live. Solomon said to keep our hearts *"with all diligence,"* for everything in life comes out of them. (See Proverbs 4:23.)

I cannot write what I am trying to communicate in this book directly onto your heart. I can only put it in print—which is something outside of you. Maybe you will understand it and maybe you will not. However, the Holy Spirit is able to write this message on your heart in a way that will change your life. Likewise, none of us by our own efforts, theology, or ministry can change one single person. But if the Holy Spirit works, He will write on the hearts of those to whom we minister, and they will be changed. That is the difference; law is external, grace is internal.

In Romans 8:14, Paul writes, *"For as many as are led by the Spirit of God, these are sons of God."* Once you have been born again, the only way to become a mature son or daughter of God is to be led by the Holy Spirit. There is no other path to maturity.

MAP OR GUIDE?

What follows is an illustration of how the Holy Spirit works in our lives. God says to you, "I am sending you on a journey, and you've got two options: you can have a perfect map, or you can have a personal guide."

The map is the law; the personal guide is the Holy Spirit. You are young, strong, and healthy, and you have two degrees from a university. So you reply to God, "Give me the map. I can read maps; I'll make it."

Two days later, it is raining hard in the middle of the night, and you are in pitch darkness on the edge of a precipice. You have no idea whether you're facing north, south, east, or west. In that desperate situation, you hear a gentle voice saying, "Can I help you?"

It is the Holy Spirit, and you respond, "O Holy Spirit, I need You. Help me!"

The Holy Spirit leads you out of that mess. You get onto the road, morning comes, the sun begins to shine, and you think, "I was pretty dumb. I didn't have to get so panicky. I think I'll have another look at the map."

You unfold your map, and when you do, your Guide is no longer there. So you carry on with the map, and a few days later you find yourself in the middle of a bog. With every step you take, you are sinking deeper. You say to yourself, *What do I do now? I can't ask the Guide back.*

However, He returns to you and says, "Let Me help you again."

That really is the story of the Christian life. How many times do we go back to the map—the law, with its rules and principles—when we can have the Guide? You may be afraid of doing the wrong thing if you don't follow the law. But let me assure you of one promise: *The Holy Spirit will never lead you to do the wrong thing.* If you are truly led by the Holy Spirit, you will always do the right thing.

God has made an escape for us from the obligations of the law through the death of Christ on the cross. Our old man was crucified with Christ—this is a statement of historical fact. Paul makes it specific and personal when he says, *"I through the law died to the law that I might live to God"* (Galatians 2:19). In view of our deliverance from the law by the cross, we have the freedom to take Paul's statement and, by our confession, make it specific for each of us.

Before we go on to the next chapter, let's confess out loud this powerful statement: "Through the law I died to the law, so that I might live to God."

Now, heave a deep sigh and say, "Thank You, Father God."

CHAPTER 11

FREEDOM FROM SELF

In the last two chapters, we have seen how the cross delivers us from this present evil age and from the demands of the law. In the passage we are studying from Galatians 2, Paul immediately presents us with a third deliverance that the cross accomplishes for us, one that is very significant. It is *our deliverance from "self."*

> *I have been crucified with Christ; it is no longer I who live, but Christ lives in me; and the life which I now live in the flesh I live by faith in the Son of God, who loved me and gave Himself for me.* (Galatians 2:20)

The cross delivers us from the tyranny of our old ego. *Ego* is the Latin word for "I." Being set free from the tyranny of ego is as important as any other deliverance mentioned in Galatians. The Greek uses the perfect tense, *"I have been crucified."* This means that even though our death was accomplished when Christ was crucified, it is not just something that happened way back in history. Rather, it is something that is a continuing state of being for us. I am permanently and continuously crucified with Christ; I have come to the end of myself.

AMBITION, PRIDE, AND SELF-CENTEREDNESS

As we discussed previously, you may have discovered—along with many of your brothers and sisters in Christ—that God sometimes must use a very hard road to bring us to the end of ourselves. Like many others, you may sometimes become disturbed and upset, complaining, "God, what are You doing with me?" The answer is simple: He is bringing us to the place where Galatians 2:20 is genuinely true in our lives. When I am crucified with Christ, I have come to the end of "me."

For our purposes in this book, I would interpret "me" as *pride* (again, in the sense of haughtiness or arrogance), *selfish ambition*, and *self-centeredness*. These are by far the most common problems within Christian ministry today. I do not want to be negative, but I don't believe there is a single person in ministry, including myself, who is excluded from these tendencies. Each one of us called by God to minister to His people needs to be continually on guard against those three related dangers: pride, selfish ambition, and self-centeredness. (Please understand that when I talk here about pride and selfish ambition, I am not referring to self-respect, or to the legitimate pleasure we take in our personal accomplishments and the accomplishments of our family members, or to a healthy ambition that motivates us to serve; I am referring to excessive conceit or self-absorption that disregards other people rather than affirms and serves them.)

Like most ministers, I have dealt with all sorts of people and their problems. In many cases, the people I meet are running away from their problems. They may be running away from their spouse, their job, or some other particularly difficult situation. Here is what I have discovered. Often, the real problem is one that none of us can run away from. It is the one we take with us wherever we go—*ourselves*.

We must all come to grips with pride, selfish ambition, and self-centeredness. How do we come to grips with it? The only way to get free from the problem of "me" is through the cross.

I have come to the conclusion that pride is a key culprit among Christians. Nobody in the Christian life goes into error except through pride—and I see countless Christians going into different sorts of error. Pride was the first sin in the history of the universe. Interestingly, that first sin did not take place on earth. It took place in heaven, in the full light of eternity and God's glory. The fact that pride is so blatant and so prevalent is a frightening thought.

If pride could break through in the very presence of God, how much easier is it for pride to break through here on earth? Somebody once said to me—and I think it is worth bearing in mind: "Pride is a sin about which Satan never makes you feel guilty."

One of the main manifestations of pride is self-centeredness. Because of my own background, I understand something of the problem of self-centeredness. I was an only child, so I never experienced learning to live with brothers or sisters. I was blessed with a good brain, and I was always successful at school and in college. Basically, I expected to be number one at everything I did—and I relied completely upon myself up to the age of twenty-five. Within limits, I did a good job.

Then God revealed Himself to me and started to change me, beginning one night in 1941 with a radical work that totally redirected me. From that new start, I made a U-turn, and I have been going in a different direction ever since.

BEYOND MY ABILITY

As I have seen the Lord totally change the direction of my life, I have come to appreciate that God has a sense of humor. About five years after I was saved, I married a Danish lady in Jerusalem who had a children's home. Not only did I get a wife, but I also acquired eight daughters in one day! Now, girls were like a strange, remote race to me; I didn't understand them. Consequently, you would have needed to look a long way to find anybody less qualified by background than I was for the position of being a father to eight girls. Prior to that occurrence, God had been dealing with my self-reliance. It seems He deliberately put me in a situation where I had little or nothing from my background to rely upon!

Let me describe the kind of person I used to be. Every time I was confronted with a problem, my first reaction was always, "What am *I* going to do about it?" By God's grace, I have come to the place of learning that my solution is not important. Rather, I have found it always best to ask, *"What is God's answer?"* I will admit this—it took a long while for me to get to that point.

I am in the ministry because God has put me here. As long as it pleases Him to keep me here, I will continue. When He is done with me, however, I am not hanging on to anything—as far as I know. By God's grace, I have experienced the power of the cross to deliver me from myself.

THE OPPOSITE MOTIVATION

In Philippians 2:3–4, Paul provides a picture of behavior that is the exact opposite of self-centeredness.

> *Let nothing be done through selfish ambition or conceit, but in lowliness of mind let each esteem others better than himself. Let each of you look out not only for his own interests, but also for the interests of others.*

"Let nothing be done through selfish ambition or conceit." I wonder how many of the current activities in the church would cease immediately if that rule were to be followed. How much ministry is motivated by selfish ambition and the desire to be recognized? I do not say this to be critical, but I believe selfish ambition and conceit are problems that are corrupting the life of the church. The only way to deal with ambition and conceit is by the cross. There is no other means.

In the previous two verses, Paul states the alternative to personal ambition:

> *Therefore if there is any consolation in Christ, if any comfort of love, if any fellowship of the Spirit, if any affection and mercy, fulfill my joy by being like-minded, having the*

same love, being of one accord, of one mind.

(Philippians 2:1–2)

Love, fellowship, affection, and mercy are beautiful expressions—and we would all love to see them flourishing in our churches. However, we first have to realize that these qualities are incompatible with selfishness and self-centeredness.

In the first four verses of Philippians 2, Paul contrasts exact opposites. Verses 1 and 2 (love, fellowship, affection, and mercy) are what we would like to enjoy. But verses 3 and 4 (selfish ambition and conceit) are what we very frequently experience in ourselves and in others. Until we come to the cross and accept God's death sentence upon "me," we will never have a solution to these problems. There is no other way to deal with them except through the cross.

A SIGN OF THE TIMES

In 2 Timothy 3, Paul paints a vivid picture of what human character and behavior will be like in the last days. He lists eighteen specific ethical and moral blemishes that will be characteristic of human culture as the end of the age draws near.

Having lived more than a few decades, I can remember the way things used to be quite a long way back. Growing up in Great Britain between the two world wars, I would say that Britain, although by no means a Christian nation, was basically a law-abiding society. However, when I talk to British young people about what it was like in those days, they cannot believe that I am telling the truth.

In my early years in ministry, I visited Sweden for the first time in 1947. At that time, I regarded Sweden as the most God-fearing nation I had ever visited. You could sense the fear of God in the streets. The people lined up in the streets on Sunday morning to get into the churches. Basically, you could trust the people to be absolutely honest and true to their commitments.

In 1983, I was again in Sweden, and I was interviewed by a young Swedish journalist who was a Christian and who asked about my background. When I told him what I remembered of Sweden slightly less than four decades earlier, he could not believe I was describing his own nation, so rapid and so radical had been the moral and ethical slide in Sweden.

I must say that this same degeneration is going on all over the world; and it is taking place with amazing rapidity. What we are presently seeing was precisely described by Paul in 2 Timothy. The Bible speaks very plainly and never indulges in wishful thinking. Its promises are true, and its warnings are equally true. As you read the passage that follows, I invite you to consider how much of what you read is manifest in our contemporary culture.

> *But know this, that in the last days perilous times will come: for men will be lovers of themselves, lovers of money, boasters, proud, blasphemers, disobedient to parents, unthankful, unholy, unloving, unforgiving, slanderers, without self-control, brutal, despisers of good, traitors, headstrong, haughty, lovers of pleasure rather than lovers of*

God, having a form of godliness but denying its power.
(2 Timothy 3:1–5)

An alternate translation for *"perilous times"* is "times of stress." That rendering is remarkable, because fifty years ago, there was not a lot of discussion about stress. Today, doctors say that stress underlies all sorts of ailments. Thus, a significant change has taken place in the last half century. The reason for perilous times is not the economy, nuclear proliferation, or terrorism. The reason exists inside human beings.

"LOVERS OF THEMSELVES"

How many of the features Paul lists in the above passage are conspicuous in our contemporary culture? We cannot say these problems are limited to any one nation. They are all over the earth. Their root cause is in the first statement: *"Men will be lovers of themselves"* (2 Timothy 3:2). Self-love (in the sense of self-absorption, or conceit) gives rise to all these other problems. We might be tempted to think that the people Paul mentions are not Christians. But Paul specifically says of them, *"Having a form of godliness…"* (2 Timothy 3:5).

Paul would never have used the word *"godliness"* of a non-Christian religion. Clearly, these are people who have a form of Christianity, but they deny its power. And when they deny the power—they deny the One who can change selfish people. What is that power? It is the power of the cross. Instead of looking to that power for deliverance from self, they rely on self-help programs, lists of rules, psychology, and so forth.

It is easy for Christians to be very respectable. They may be able to abstain from drugs, alcohol, illicit sex, and all the obvious sins. They may pay their debts. They may be good church members and law-abiding citizens who don't even break the traffic laws. Yet, they may be very self-centered people. People like this have a form of godliness, yet they deny—or resist—the power of the cross to change them radically. Until *self* is dealt with, we have not been changed radically.

DEALING WITH THE ROOT

The word *radical* is derived from the Latin word *radix*, which means "root." Radical is that which goes to the root. John the Baptist introduced the gospel and Jesus by declaring, "*Now the ax is laid to the root of the trees. Therefore every tree which does not bear good fruit is cut down and thrown into the fire*" (Matthew 3:10).

The gospel of the kingdom of God is the most radical message that has ever confronted humanity. It deals with root issues—the chief of which is *selfishness*, or *self-love*. The only ax that will cut through that root is the cross.

When I became involved in the ministry of deliverance from demons in the 1960s, I began to work with obvious sins like addiction to nicotine, alcohol, and drugs. I soon discovered, however, that I was only dealing with small branches that grew on bigger branches. For instance, one of the bigger branches is frustration. Every addiction grows out of a frustration. If you have not dealt with the frustration, you have not really solved the larger basic problem of the addiction.

As my involvement in the deliverance ministry progressed, I realized that I was dealing with the bigger branches, but I was not getting to the trunk of the tree. You can cut down a lot of branches, but if the trunk is not severed, the tree will go on growing more of the same branches.

Finally, God showed me I had to deal with the root—which consists of self-love, selfishness, and self-centeredness. Until the root has been addressed, we really cannot have the benefits of the gospel that God intends us to have. Self-love and the Christ-nature are opposites. We must let self-love die so that the Christ-nature can move in to take its place.

THE PROCESS OF DENYING OURSELVES

In dealing with personal issues like these, I encourage people to be realistic about themselves and not overestimate their spirituality. It is never my intention to bring anybody under condemnation, because God is gracious, merciful, and patient. But it is also imperative that you do not deceive yourself, thinking that you are beyond where you really are spiritually. It is important for you to check on how much self-love, selfishness, and self-centeredness still dominate your life. Measuring those components will give you the answer to where you are spiritually.

In Matthew 16:24–25, Jesus revealed the first steps to following Him:

> *Then Jesus said to His disciples, "If anyone desires to come after Me, let him deny himself, and take up his cross, and*

*follow Me. For whoever desires to save his life will lose it,
but whoever loses his life for My sake will find it."*

If you want to follow Jesus, the essential first step is *the
denial of self.* What does Jesus mean when He says we must
deny ourselves? To deny is to say no. Therefore, if you want to
follow Jesus, the first step is to say no to yourself.

The original Greek literally says *to deny your soul.*
Generally speaking, there are three aspects to the soul: the
will, the intellect, and the emotions. The will says, "I want";
the intellect says, "I think"; and the emotions say, "I feel."

Therefore, when you deny yourself, you say, "It's not what
I want, it's God's will." "It's not what I think, it's what God
says." "It's not what I feel, it's what the Holy Spirit impresses
upon me." These are three areas where we must deny ourselves.
When we have denied ourselves in these ways, we can begin to
follow Jesus.

Jesus says the second step is *the taking up of your cross.* God
does not impose the cross on us. He did not impose the cross
on Jesus. Jesus took up His own cross. Here are two defini-
tions of a personal cross. First, your cross is the place where
God's will and your will cross. Second, your cross is the place
where you die.

Again, taking up and embracing your cross is your decision. You are not forced to do it. It is a step you can refuse. But
according to Jesus, you cannot take the third step of *following
Him* until you have done it. If you want to come after Him,
you must first deny yourself. Then you must take up your

cross, which is the place where you will die to self-love and self-centeredness.

God has a specific cross for each one of us. As with Jesus, it is your decision whether to take it up. But the truth is, you cannot advance any further without making this decision.

After we have taken these steps, we can begin to say, as Paul did in Philippians 4:13, *"I can do all things through Christ who strengthens me."* I prefer to translate this verse in the following way: "I can do all things through the One who empowers me within." You cannot receive His power within as long as you are operating in your self-life. By God's grace, the cross has provided deliverance for you and me from the tyranny of self-centeredness.

Recognizing our profound freedom through the cross, this would be a wonderful time to repeat what we did at the end of the previous chapter: heave a deep sigh of relief and say, "Thank You, Father God!"

CHAPTER 12

FREEDOM FROM THE FLESH

The fourth area of our lives from which the cross provides deliverance is what the Scripture calls *"the flesh."* In Galatians 5:24, Paul writes, *"Those who are Christ's have crucified the flesh with its passions and desires."*

THE NATURE OF A REBEL

We need to understand that references in Scripture to *"the flesh"* are not primarily about our physical body. "The flesh" is the *nature* you and I received when we were born in a physical body. It is essentially the nature of a rebel, which has all sorts of desires and feelings that are not in line with God's will.

Notice that Paul said, *"Those who are Christ's have crucified the flesh...."*

People who belong to Jesus Christ are not a denomination or a particular religious group, such as Baptists, charismatics, or Catholics. Those who are Christ's are marked out and distinguished from others as people who have crucified the flesh.

In 1 Corinthians 15:23, Paul says that the individuals who will be counted in the resurrection are *"those who are Christ's at*

His coming." And again, an important mark of the people who are Christ's is that they have crucified the flesh. We can sum this up by stating that Jesus is coming back for Christians who *"have crucified the flesh with its passions and desires."*

·I vividly remember the prayer of a lady in our church in London many years ago. One of her regular prayers was, "Lord, help us to remember that the time of Your return will be too late for us to be getting ready."

I have never forgotten that. We cannot leave preparation for the Lord's return to the last moment. The last moment will be too late. We must have already dealt with the flesh.

IN DIRECT OPPOSITION

The fleshly nature is in direct opposition to the will and the ways of God. In Romans 8, Paul says that *"the carnal mind is enmity against God."* The word *"carnal"* means the same as "fleshly." It is simply a different English word, derived from the Latin root *carnalis*.

> The carnal [fleshly] *mind is enmity against God; for it is not subject to the law of God, nor indeed can be. So then, those who are in the flesh cannot please God.*
>
> (Romans 8:7–8)

Anyone who is controlled by the fleshly nature cannot please God. We can try as hard as we might, we can be as religious as we please, but nothing that originates from our flesh will ever be acceptable to God.

Paul presents this truth again in Galatians 5:17:

For the flesh lusts against the Spirit, and the Spirit against the flesh; and these are contrary to one another, so that you do not do the things that you wish.

Our natural, fleshly desires are contrary to the will and the ways of the Spirit of God. This may be new information for you, so it's best to take note of it. Again, you can approach God with all sorts of good spiritual intentions to live wholly for Him. You can attempt to consecrate yourself. You can even go forward to the altar of the church and pray a nice prayer to that effect. You may then say to yourself, "That takes care of that. Now, I'm going to do this or that for God."

However, a few weeks later, you wonder how you could ever have gotten so far away from what you intended to be and do! Here is the explanation: *"the flesh lusts against the Spirit."* Working in you is an enemy of God—your fleshly nature. That enemy has to be dealt with through the cross. Until we have *"crucified the flesh with its passions and desires"* (Galatians 5:24), we cannot successfully lead the Christian life.

IS IT ONLY ME?

It may be encouraging for you to know that Paul himself had the same problem. Struggling against the fleshly nature is not a battle that just a few weak people face. It is universal in every human being. If you read Romans 7, you will see Paul's personal struggles against the flesh. It has been my observation that the most dedicated Christians—and the ones whom God intends to use the most—are the ones who have the most struggles.

Many Christians have adopted the attitude that if you are saved, baptized in water, baptized in the Spirit, and speak in tongues, you will have no more problems. Have you discovered it does not work that way? I wish what those Christians believe were really true, but I know it does not work that way. At least, that's not the way it has worked for me. I have pastored long enough to find out the reason it does not work. That reason is the flesh—pure and simple—because the flesh is an enemy of God.

Here is what Paul says in Romans 7:15 about his own experience:

> *For what I am doing, I do not understand. For what I will to do, that I do not practice; but what I hate, that I do.*

Was Paul unique in this experience? No, he was not. The same is true of all of us. None of us can point a finger at somebody else, believing that Paul's dilemma applies only to them. Each of us must look in the mirror and admit that it applies to us as well. Paul explains why this happens. The reason? *"Because the carnal mind is enmity against God; for it is not subject to the law of God, nor indeed can be"* (Romans 8:7).

RELIGION DOESN'T HELP

Many people may be surprised to learn that religion will not solve this dilemma. Religion, as opposed to the work of the Holy Spirit, is a system that uses rules to try to make the flesh behave. Religion can make the flesh religious, but it does not have the power to make the flesh acceptable to God. Religious people are simply suppressing the flesh. They are forcing their flesh to conform outwardly, while their inward attitude of rebellion remains unchanged.

In Galatians 5:19–21, Paul lists the results of the legalism and carnality that were rampant among the Galatians:

> Now the works of the flesh are evident, which are: adultery, fornication, uncleanness, lewdness, idolatry, sorcery, hatred, contentions, jealousies, outbursts of wrath, selfish ambitions, dissensions, heresies, envy, murders, drunkenness, revelries, and the like; of which I tell you beforehand, just as I also told you in time past, that those who practice such things will not inherit the kingdom of God.

If you analyze the works of the flesh included in this passage, you will find they fall into four categories:

First, sexual immorality. This includes adultery, fornication, uncleanness, and licentiousness. Many people believe sexual immorality is the major work of the flesh. Some even believe it is the only area that needs to be dealt with. However, sexuality immorality is by no means the greatest problem.

The second area is the occult. This includes idolatry and sorcery, or, as the King James Version reads, "witchcraft." Clearly, these are works of the flesh. But when the flesh indulges in these practices, it opens the door to demonic affliction.

The initial motivation for idolatry and witchcraft is rooted in the fleshly nature. Witchcraft is humanity's way of trying to control people and get them to comply. Any attempt to control others is the beginning of witchcraft. When that process continues and deepens, it becomes demonic.

The third and largest category in the list of the works of the flesh is wrong attitudes and relationships. Paul lists hatred, contentions, jealousies, outbursts of wrath, selfish ambitions, dissensions, heresies, and envy. These are various descriptions of wrong attitudes and wrong relationships. We need to recognize that these problems are just as much sins of the flesh as adultery or fornication is. Generally, religious people ignore or even condone these works of the flesh—while, at the same time, aligning themselves strictly against all forms of sexual immorality.

The final category is what I call "sensual self-indulgence." This category includes drunkenness, revelries, "and the like." In a way, it is irrelevant how any of these practices are categorized. In the broadest sense, they are all different expressions of our fleshly nature and can be dealt with only by the cross. Thankfully, as stated at the beginning of this chapter, the power of the cross working in us brings deliverance from the flesh.

THE CAUSE OF ALL DIVISION

Turning to yet another problem produced by the flesh, in 1 Corinthians 3, Paul pinpoints the cause of divisions in the church—the carnal nature. Until the carnal nature is dealt with through the cross, we will always have division in the body of Christ. Paul writes to the Corinthian Christians:

You are still carnal. For where there are envy, strife, and divisions among you, are you not carnal and behaving like mere men? For when one says, "I am of Paul," and another, "I am of Apollos," are you not carnal?

(1 Corinthians 3:3–4)

How did Paul know the Corinthians were carnal, or fleshly? The mere fact that there were divisions and strife was sufficient evidence to recognize they were operating in the flesh. Furthermore, he knew there were divisions among them because some were saying, "*I am of Paul,*" and others, "*I am of Apollos.*"

As long as we are divided by following human leaders rather than Christ, we are carnal. Paul did not say it was acceptable to follow Paul but not acceptable to follow Apollos. He said it was wrong to fall into divisive allegiance to any human leader.

Among Christians today, some people will say, "I am of Luther," or "I am of Wesley," or "I am of Calvin," or they will say they are of some pastor or special teacher. Any Christians who make some individual or teaching their first commitment fall into this category.

Many people think doctrine is the cause of division. But that's not true. It is carnality that causes division. Of course, theology can be used carnally to divide the body. But the root cause of division in the body of Christ is the flesh—for which the only solution is the cross.

APPLYING GOD'S SOLUTION

What is the solution God has provided for these persistent problems with the flesh? Paul states it very clearly in Romans 6:6:

> *Knowing this, that our old man was crucified with Him, that the body of sin might be done away with, that we should no longer be slaves of sin.*

As we noted in an earlier chapter about deliverance from the law, God's provision is *execution*. He has made that provision for us in our identification with the death of Jesus. But here is our biggest challenge: we must learn how to apply the solution God has provided for us.

Christ has done His part, but we must add to His work our application of that work. We see some helpful insights in 1 Peter 4:1–2:

> *Therefore, since Christ suffered for us in the flesh, arm yourselves also with the same mind, for he who has suffered in the flesh has ceased from sin, that he no longer should live the rest of his time in the flesh for the lusts of men, but for the will of God.*

Peter outlines a principle here that is rather surprising to most of us: "He who has suffered in the flesh has ceased from sin." For a long while, I wondered about that statement. Here was my thinking: *If Jesus suffered on my behalf, why should I have to suffer?* I believe the Lord helped me to see that Jesus has made the provision, but we must apply it.

Remember that according to Galatians 5:24, *"those who are Christ's have crucified the flesh."* God does not crucify us. We must do it ourselves—and any way you look at it, crucifixion is painful. What must we do to crucify our fleshly nature? We have to take hold of our evil, rebellious desires and attitudes and nail them to the cross.

You and I must take the nails of Scripture and drive them through our own hands and feet in order to put that rebel in us to death. You and I must do that. It is not done for us. It is painful—but it is the way out of sin.

A PRACTICAL EXAMPLE

Here is an example that may make this principle easier to understand. Consider a fine young lady about twenty years old who is a committed Christian. She is a member of a good fellowship of believers. She has a pastor who is a godly man and who really cares about her soul.

In time, she becomes emotionally involved with a man who is not a committed Christian. This man goes to church with her just to placate her. But really, he has never committed his life to Christ. The lady's pastor has told her not to get involved with him because he is not a committed Christian, warning that the relationship may not work out well for her.

She now has two options, each of which is painful. She can accept her pastor's advice and nail her feelings and desires to the cross. In that case, she will say, "I love him, but that's not the most important thing. I want to be married, but that's not the most important thing either. I'm afraid of being lonely, but that, also, is not the most important thing."

Every one of those desires and attitudes has to be nailed to the cross. It is painful for her, but the pain does not last forever. After a little while, there is a glorious freedom. Of course, we could project a happy ending to the story: in due course, the man comes to Christ, the young lady marries him, and they live happily ever after. That would be the happy ending most people would hope for. However, regardless of what the man does or does not do, the young woman must take the steps of nailing her desires to the cross. Only then will she be free.

Now let's suppose she does not go to the cross with her feelings—she does not crucify her attitudes, her desires, and her emotions. She marries this man, and fifteen years later, after she has had three children, he walks out on her for another woman. Then she must pick up the pieces of her life and handle a family without a husband for her or a father for her children.

This ending is far more painful. And it lasts far longer. Hopefully, at the end of this scenario, she learns her lesson and sees that she was self-willed and self-pleasing. She gave way to her flesh and did not accept the cross.

One time, I was giving this example to a gathering of believers, and a lady who was right in the front row said, "You've just told my story exactly." She had just been divorced, and her husband had left her and their six children. I am not suggesting that all divorce springs from this cause. But I think it is fair to say that a lot of unhappy marriages of Christians are the result of not crucifying the flesh.

Here is my challenge to you: Are you going to take God's solution, which is painful (and truly, it *is painful* to deny your strongest desires and wishes and feelings)? Or are you going to refuse the cross and suffer the consequences, which will be, in the long run, much more painful? This is the decision we each must make.

A STEP YOU CAN TAKE

As we close this chapter, something may be stirring inside your heart. Maybe you are facing a situation very similar to the one just described. It may not be a romantic entanglement—but it is an area of your life where you know the flesh is winning out. This could be your moment to begin the process of nailing those fleshly desires and attitudes to the cross.

Ask yourself if you are ready to begin that process today. The issue you face may not be totally resolved through the prayer we are about to offer together. But at least you can tell the Lord that you are willing to take the first steps. Will you join me in a prayer to that end?

Lord, I know You are putting Your finger on an area I need to deal with. Please help me at this moment. I bring this matter before Your throne. In Your presence, I recognize it for what it is: a work of the flesh that is a barrier in the path of my relationship with You. By faith, I place it on the cross, and I drive in the first nail to sacrifice it and give it up. In doing so, I declare the truth I have learned in this chapter: those who are Yours have crucified the flesh with its passions and desires. By faith, I proclaim that the cross of Jesus Christ will provide my deliverance from this and every work of the flesh in my life. Amen!

CHAPTER 13

FREEDOM FROM THE WORLD

The fifth and final deliverance we are going to explore is *deliverance from the world*. Paul expresses this deliverance in the following way:

> But God forbid that I should boast except in the cross of our Lord Jesus Christ, by whom the world has been crucified to me, and I to the world. (Galatians 6:14)

First, we must define *"the world"* as it is used in this verse. "Worldly" is one of those terms Christians use to criticize other Christians and to condemn non-Christians. However, that is not God's purpose or desire. I believe a good, workable definition of "the world" would be this: *The world is a social order or a system of life that refuses the righteous government of Jesus Christ.* This statement recognizes, as a matter of prime importance, that Jesus is God's appointed Governor and Ruler of the human race.

Thus, the world is a system, or an attitude, that refuses the righteous government of Jesus. Worldly people can be religious, nice, and respectable. Often, however, when you challenge these same people with the need for unreserved submission to the lordship of Jesus, an attitude of self-will and rebellion manifests. That is *the world.*

CALLED OUT OF THE WORLD

Here are a few truths from the New Testament concerning the world as defined in the above context. In John 15:18–19, Jesus uses the phrase *"the world"* six times when He says to His disciples,

> *If the world hates you, you know that it hated Me before it hated you. If you were of the world, the world would love its own. Yet because you are not of the world, but I chose you out of the world, therefore the world hates you.*

Jesus has chosen us out of the world. The word for *"church"* in New Testament Greek is *ekklesia,* which means "a company of people called out." In the case of the church, it is a group of people called out from the world. We can be either *in the world* or *in the church.* But we cannot be in both. They are mutually exclusive.

The apostle John writes about the attractiveness and glamour of the world:

> *Do not love the world or the things in the world. If anyone loves the world, the love of the Father is not in him. For all that is in the world—the lust of the flesh, the lust of the eyes, and the pride of life—is not of the Father but is of the world. And the world is passing away, and the lust of it; but he who does the will of God abides forever.*
>
> (1 John 2:15–17)

Do you love the world? This matter of whether or not we love the world is the question of this age. For most of us, especially when we are young, it is a great temptation to love the world. It seems so glamorous and exciting. It seems to have so much to offer. However, all the world's glamour is tinsel; there is no reality to it.

As we become older, our problem is not so much loving the world as loving what we have acquired from the world—like a special car, a larger house, or the wardrobe we have collected. There is just something powerful that draws us to those possessions.

Older, more mature people usually become somewhat disillusioned with the world. Yet even when we reach a later age, there is still a powerful attraction to the world that holds on to us. It may be something in our intellectual, sentimental, philosophical, or religious background that strengthens the force of the world to hold on to our mind and emotions.

OVERCOMING THE WORLD'S ATTRACTION

All of us struggle against the attraction of the world, including myself. One of the disciplines I use in order to combat this is that I try never to fill my mind with worldly garbage. If I think something is unhealthy for my mind, I close my mind to it and shut it off. I do not want to carry garbage in my mind. Many Christians who would never indulge in immorality or sensuality indulge in intellectual garbage. That is one way the world still holds on to their lives.

In John's first epistle quoted earlier, the apostle says we cannot love the world and God the Father at the same time. We must choose—because everything in the world is not of God the Father. In this world system that attracts our attention, John mentions three specific types of temptation: *"the lust of the flesh, the lust of the eyes, and the pride of life"* (1 John 2:16).

In the original temptation in the garden of Eden, all three of these temptations were present. The fruit on the tree was good for food: it tasted good to the flesh. The fruit looked good: it was pleasant to the eyes. The fruit was desirable to make one wise: this appealed to the pride of life. (See Genesis 2:15–17; 3:1–7.) The pride of life is very clever. It tells us, "I can handle life on my own. I don't need God."

The essence of the sin Adam and Eve committed did not spring from a desire to do evil. Actually, the temptation—subtle and powerful—was for something good: to be like God, knowing good and evil. There is nothing wrong with that desire in itself. However, for Adam and Eve in their disobedience, it reflected the essence of sin, which is the desire *to be independent of God*. That desire is the pride of life. As long as there is anything in us that resists depending on God, the pride of life has not been dealt with in us.

John says, *"And the world is passing away, and the lust of it; but he who does the will of God abides forever"* (1 John 2:17). That is an exciting statement. Everything in this world is impermanent—it will not last. But if we will renounce the things of the world and align our will totally with the will of God, then we are as unshakeable, undefeatable, and unsinkable as the will of

God. If we will align ourselves with God's purposes, there is nothing that can defeat us, because there is nothing that can defeat the will of God.

Here, then, are the options before us: We can stay embroiled with the world and suffer its miseries. Or, we can turn our backs on the world, align ourselves with the will of God, and become unshakeable, unsinkable, and undefeatable.

In 1 John 5:19, the apostle makes a sweeping statement: *"We know that we are of God, and the whole world lies under the sway of the wicked one."* In the original Greek, the last part of the verse is expressed in even simpler terms. It says, *"...the whole world lies in the wicked one."* The wicked one is Satan. The whole world is under the sway of Satan.

In Revelation 12:9, Satan is called the *"great dragon,"* the *"serpent of old,"* the *"Devil"* (the slanderer), and *"Satan"* (the adversary), *"who deceives the whole world."* We must understand that the whole world is under the deception of Satan. Additionally, we need to remember that we cannot love God and the world simultaneously. James wrote,

> *Adulterers and adulteresses! Do you not know that friendship with the world is enmity with God? Whoever therefore wants to be a friend of the world makes himself an enemy of God.* (James 4:4)

THE FIFTH COLUMN

Jesus said, *"The ruler of this world* [Satan] *is coming, and he has nothing in Me"* (John 14:30). In relation to this statement, I want to give one more illustration as we close this chapter. The question you and I must ask ourselves is whether or not Satan has anything "in us." Or, to put it another way, do we have a fifth column in us that is in league with the enemy?

The origin of the term "fifth column" is interesting. Between 1936 and 1939, there was a civil war in Spain. General Emilio Mola told a journalist that he had four columns of troops that were approaching Madrid, ready to capture the city. He also said he had a "fifth column" of followers inside the city who would support him and undermine the enemy forces inside the city.

Similarly, the church will never be defeated from without. You and I will never be defeated by any outside forces. However, if there is a "fifth column" inside us, that is how we can be defeated. Jesus said, in effect, "The ruler of this world has nothing (no fifth column) inside of Me." The same must be true of us.

A little parable about a ship and the sea illustrates this reality very clearly:

A ship in the sea is all right.
The sea in a ship is all wrong.

What is the application? The church in the world is all right; the world in the church is all wrong. When the sea gets into a ship, the ship sinks. When the world gets into the church, the church sinks. The only remedy—the only force that can free us from the world's grip and bring deliverance to us—is the cross.

These, then, are the five primary deliverances provided by the cross as described in Galatians:

+ from this present evil age
+ from the law as a means of righteousness
+ from self
+ from the flesh
+ from the world

AFFIRMING OUR FREEDOMS THROUGH THE CROSS

I believe it would be helpful for us to end this chapter with an affirmation of the freedoms the cross brings to us—a culmination of applying what we have learned over the last few chapters in a very practical way. Earlier in the book, we made two proclamations. Let's confess both of these again to affirm our freedoms—every deliverance purchased for us by Jesus at Calvary. Let's speak them out loud and boldly declare Jesus' total victory over Satan through the cross.

Confessing the Power of the Blood

Through the blood of Jesus, I am redeemed out of the hand of the devil.[1]

Through the blood of Jesus, all my sins are forgiven.[2]

Through the blood of Jesus, I am continually being cleansed from all sin.[3]

Through the blood of Jesus, I am justified, made righteous, just-as-if-I'd never sinned.[4]

Through the blood of Jesus, I am sanctified, made holy, set apart to God.[5]

Through the blood of Jesus, I have boldness to enter into the presence of God.[6]

Through the blood of Jesus, I overcome the work of Satan.[7]

The blood of Jesus cries out continually to God in heaven on my behalf.[8]

[1]Ephesians 1:7; 1 Peter 1:19. [2]Ephesians 1:7. [3]1 John 1:7. [4]Romans 5:9. [5]Hebrews 13:12. [6]Hebrews 10:19. [7]Revelation 12:11. [8]Hebrews 12:24.

Confessing the Truths of Revelation 12:11

And now the second proclamation, drawn extensively from Revelation 12:11:

My body is a temple for the Holy Spirit; redeemed, cleansed, and sanctified by the blood of Jesus. My members, the parts of my body, are instruments of righteousness, yielded to God for His service and for His glory. The devil has no place in me, no power over me, no unsettled claims against me. All has been settled by the blood of Jesus. I overcome Satan by the blood of the Lamb and by the word of my testimony, and I love not my life unto the death. My body is for the Lord, and the Lord is for my body.

Once again, I would recommend making these confessions regularly. It is a very practical way for us to apply the victory that Jesus won over Satan at the cross. To help in this matter, you will find these two proclamations in a separate section at the back of this book so you may easily refer to them.

CHAPTER 14

COMING TO THE CROSS

I would like to conclude this book with an example of the work of the cross from my own life. This illustration, along with the prayer offered at the end of the chapter, will help us to know how practical the application of the cross is to all of our needs.

MY ENCOUNTER WITH CHRIST

I had a dramatic personal encounter with the Lord Jesus Christ in the summer of 1941 while serving as a lance corporal in the British army. At the time, I was a confused person. I had been a student of philosophy, but I had grown weary of philosophic theories. In essence, I had searched everywhere I knew for answers to life without finding any.

However, in just one encounter with Jesus Christ, the whole course of my life was completely, radically, and permanently changed. From the morning after that encounter onward, I was a totally different person. Bear in mind, I was not a perfect person—but I was a different person. Truly, I have never been the same since.

"CONSIDER THE WORK OF CALVARY"

For the next three years, the army sent me into the deserts of Egypt, Libya, and the Sudan. While in the desert, I developed a skin condition that the doctors in those days and in that climate were not able to cure. As a result, I spent almost exactly one year in military hospitals in Egypt.

I had been in hospital for several months when a lady who was a brigadier general in the Salvation Army came to visit me. What made her very unusual was that she was a tongues-speaking Salvation Army brigadier! She marched into the ward in her full Salvation Army attire, overawed the nurse, and obtained permission for me to go out and sit with her in her car to pray together. She did not ask me whether I wanted to pray. She just decided we were going to pray!

I found myself sitting in the backseat of a very small, four-seater car beside a young American lady from Oklahoma whom the brigadier general had brought with her. After we had been praying for a while, the young woman beside me started to speak in tongues. Not only did she speak in tongues, but she also began to vibrate.

She was shaking noticeably, and then I realized that I was shaking as well. Then I realized that everybody in the car was shaking. After that, I saw that the whole car was shaking! The car was stationary and the engine was not running—yet it was shaking as if we were traveling on a rough road at considerable speed. Instantly and intuitively, I realized God was doing all this for my benefit.

After the young lady from Oklahoma had spoken in the unknown tongue, she immediately gave the interpretation in English. I do not recall most of what she said, but there were two sentences that burned into my consciousness and have been there ever since. I knew somehow that the words were spoken to me. She said:

Consider the work of Calvary. A perfect work—
perfect in every respect, perfect in every aspect.

Having studied Greek, my mind immediately went to the Greek New Testament and the final words that Jesus spoke on the cross: "*It is finished!*" (John 19:30). Actually, the *New King James Version's* translation is inadequate, because the verb is in the perfect tense. Literally, the declaration is, "It has been finished." Again, the perfect tense of a Greek verb means to do something perfectly. You could say it is "perfectly perfect" or "completely complete."

When this young lady spoke the words "a perfect work— perfect in every respect, perfect in every aspect," I immediately knew it was the Holy Spirit's interpretation of Jesus' statement "*It is finished!*"

Then and there, I realized a truth God was showing me. He was letting me know that the answer to my need was to be found in what Jesus had done on my behalf on the cross. Beyond that, every need that could ever arise in my life had been provided for by that sacrifice of Jesus on the cross. It was perfect in every respect. It did not matter what the need might be. Whether it was spiritual or physical, material or financial, temporal or eternal—it was covered. It did not matter from what point of view I looked at the cross—it was perfect.

When I got out of that car, I was just as sick with the skin condition as I had been when I entered the car. But I knew that God had showed me where to find the answer to my needs. For the next three to five months in the hospital, I did what the Holy Spirit told me to do: *I considered the work of Calvary.*

When I had become sufficiently convinced that on the cross Jesus not only bore my sins but also took my sicknesses, then by His wounds I was healed. (See Isaiah 53:5.) After I applied this truth, I was discharged from the hospital. Within three months, I was perfectly healed. Clearly, the Lord did not want me out of the hospital until I had come face-to-face with what Jesus did for me on the cross.

Likewise, it does not matter what need you have in your life. It does not matter what your problem is. It does not matter what you are praying for. It does not matter whether it is personal or individual, or whether it covers the whole church, the whole nation, or the whole world. The cross is the only all-sufficient basis on which God will meet you and answer your prayer. Coming to God through the cross will never be in vain for you, because every need, every situation, and every problem is covered by the cross.

A PERFECT WORK

If, as you have read through this book and allowed the Word to minister to your heart, you have realized that you have not sufficiently appreciated the cross of Jesus, then I invite you to join me in the following prayer as we ask the Lord to help us. God the Father is wonderfully gracious. He is waiting for us to step forward into the place of blessing through the cross.

Father, I thank You for the cross. You have made provision for my sin in Your infinite wisdom and mercy. Thank You for sending Jesus to die for me to bring me back into relationship with You.

Forgive me for the times when I have failed to keep the cross at the center of my focus, for allowing other concerns to crowd out this most important truth. With this prayer, I choose the cross as the means to all the provision of all my needs. Please help me to move from understanding this theoretically to experiencing it personally, applying the cross to all areas of my life. Let me know the fullness of the cross as I yield to You.

Thank You for opening my eyes to the "Galatian problem" of starting in the Spirit but reverting to the flesh. Forgive me for looking to human wisdom and effort to accomplish what can be provided only through what Jesus did on the cross for me. I recognize this tendency to rely on myself as a problem in my life, and I repent, renouncing this soulish way of life as I choose instead to be led by Your Spirit. Thank You for making a way back for me into a place of freedom and blessing.

Father, You have allowed Jesus to become a curse upon the cross so that I might be redeemed from the curse—so that I might be restored to the blessing of the fullness of the Holy Spirit. Help me to grow in my understanding and application of the glorious deliverances provided through the cross:

+ Deliverance from this present evil age

+ Deliverance from the law as a means of righteousness

+ Deliverance from self

+ Deliverance from the flesh

+ Deliverance from the world

I ask now, in Jesus' name, that You would deliver me from each of these impediments. Please fill me afresh with the Holy Spirit. I commit myself to consider the work of Calvary: a perfect work—perfect in every respect, perfect in every aspect.

I close my prayer to You with this declaration from Your Word: *"God forbid that I should boast except in the cross of our Lord Jesus Christ."* Amen.

ABOUT THE AUTHOR

Derek Prince (1915–2003) was born in India of British parents. He was educated as a scholar of Greek and Latin at Eton College and King's College, Cambridge, in England. Upon graduation, he held a fellowship (equivalent to a professorship) in Ancient and Modern Philosophy at King's College. Prince also studied Hebrew, Aramaic, and modern languages at Cambridge and the Hebrew University in Jerusalem. As a student, he was a philosopher and a self-proclaimed agnostic.

While serving in the British Medical Corps during World War II, Prince began to study the Bible as a philosophical work. Converted through a powerful encounter with Jesus Christ, he was baptized in the Holy Spirit a few days later. Out of this encounter, he formed two conclusions: first, that Jesus Christ is alive; second, that the Bible is a true, relevant, up-to-date book. These conclusions altered the whole course of his life, which he then devoted to studying and teaching the Bible as the Word of God.

Discharged from the army in Jerusalem in 1945, he married Lydia Christensen, founder of a children's home there. Upon their marriage, he immediately became father to Lydia's eight adopted daughters—six Jewish, one Palestinian Arab, and one English. Together, the family saw the rebirth of the state of Israel in 1948. In the late 1950s, they adopted another daughter while Prince was serving as principal of a teachers' training college in Kenya.

In 1963, the Princes immigrated to the United States and pastored a church in Seattle. In 1973, Prince became one of the founders of Intercessors for America. His book *Shaping History through Prayer and Fasting* has awakened Christians around the world to their responsibility to pray for their governments. Many consider underground translations of the book as instrumental in the fall of communist regimes in the USSR, East Germany, and Czechoslovakia.

Lydia Prince died in 1975, and Prince married Ruth Baker (a single mother to three adopted children) in 1978. He met his second wife, like his first wife, while she was serving the Lord in Jerusalem. Ruth died in December 1998 in Jerusalem, where they had lived since 1981.

Until a few years before his own death in 2003 at the age of eighty-eight, Prince persisted in the ministry God had called him to as he traveled the world, imparting God's revealed truth, praying for the sick and afflicted, and sharing his prophetic insights into world events in the light of Scripture. Internationally recognized as a Bible scholar and spiritual patriarch, Derek Prince established a teaching ministry that spanned six continents and more than sixty years. He is the author of more than eighty books, six hundred audio teachings, and one hundred video teachings, many of which have been translated and published in more than one hundred languages. He pioneered teaching on such groundbreaking themes as generational curses, the biblical significance of Israel, and demonology.

Prince's radio program, which began in 1979, has been translated into more than a dozen languages and continues to touch lives. Derek Prince's main gift of explaining the Bible and its teachings in a clear and simple way has helped build a foundation of faith in millions of lives. His nondenominational, nonsectarian approach has made his teaching equally relevant and helpful to people from all racial and religious backgrounds, and his messages are estimated to have reached more than half the globe.

In 2002, he said, "It is my desire—and I believe the Lord's desire—that this ministry continue the work, which God began through me over sixty years ago, until Jesus returns."

Derek Prince Ministries–International continues to reach out to believers in over 140 countries with Derek's teaching, fulfilling the mandate to keep on "until Jesus returns." This is accomplished through the outreaches of more than forty-five Derek Prince offices around the world, including primary work in Australia, Canada, China, France, Germany, the Netherlands, New Zealand, Norway, Russia, South Africa, Switzerland, the United Kingdom, and the United States. For current information about these and other worldwide locations, visit www.derekprince.org.

PROCLAMATIONS ABOUT THE CROSS

CONFESSING THE POWER OF THE BLOOD

Through the blood of Jesus, I am redeemed out of the hand of the devil.[1]

Through the blood of Jesus, all my sins are forgiven.[2]

Through the blood of Jesus, I am continually being cleansed from all sin.[3]

Through the blood of Jesus, I am justified, made righteous, just-as-if-I'd never sinned.[4]

Through the blood of Jesus, I am sanctified, made holy, set apart to God.[5]

Through the blood of Jesus, I have boldness to enter into the presence of God.[6]

Through the blood of Jesus, I overcome the work of Satan.[7]

The blood of Jesus cries out continually to God in heaven on my behalf.[8]

[1]Ephesians 1:7; 1 Peter 1:19. [2]Ephesians 1:7. [3]1 John 1:7. [4]Romans 5:9. [5]Hebrews 13:12. [6]Hebrews 10:19. [7]Revelation 12:11. [8]Hebrews 12:24.

CONFESSING THE TRUTHS OF REVELATION 12:11

My body is a temple for the Holy Spirit; redeemed, cleansed, and sanctified by the blood of Jesus. My members, the parts of my body, are instruments of righteousness, yielded to God for His service and for His glory. The devil has no place in me, no power over me, no unsettled claims against me. All has been settled by the blood of Jesus. I overcome Satan by the blood of the Lamb and by the word of my testimony, and I love not my life unto the death. My body is for the Lord, and the Lord is for my body.